Matt
989 ℓ

The Practitioner Inquiry Series

Marilyn Cochran-Smith and Susan L. Lytle, SERIES EDITORS

ADVISORY BOARD: JoBeth Allen, Rebecca Barr, Judy Buchanan, Robert Fecho, Susan Florio-Ruane, Sarah Freedman, Karen Gallas, Andrew Gitlin, Dixie Goswami, Peter Grimmett, Gloria Ladson-Billings, Sarah Michaels, Susan Noffke, Marsha Pincus, Marty Rutherford, Lynne Strieb, Carol Tateishi, Diane Waff, Ken Zeichner

(continued)

"IS THIS ENGLISH?"

Race, Language, and Culture in the Classroom

Bob Fecho

FOREWORD BY

GLORIA LADSON-BILLINGS

Teachers College
Columbia University
New York and London

Published by Teachers College Press, 1234 Amsterdam Avenue, New York, NY 10027

Chapter 5 originally appeared in a somewhat altered form as Fecho, B., (2000), Critical inquiries into language in an urban classroom, *Research in the Teaching of English*, 34(3), 368–395.

Chapter 6 originally appeared in a somewhat altered form as Fecho, B., (2001), "Why are you doing this?": Acknowledging and transcending threat in critical inquiry classrooms, *Research in the Teaching of English*, 36(1), 9–37.

Chapter 7 originally appeared in a somewhat altered form as Fecho, B., with Green, A., (2002), Madaz Publications: Polyphonic identity and existential literacy transactions, *Harvard Educational Review*, 72(1), 93–119.

Library of Congress Cataloging-in-Publication Data

Fecho, Bob.
    "Is This English?" : race, language, and culture in the classroom / Bob Fecho ; foreword by Gloria Ladson-Billings.
       p. cm. — (The practitioner inquiry series)
    Includes bibliographical references (p.   ) and index.
    ISBN 0-8077-4408-5 (cloth : alk. paper) — ISBN 0-8077-4407-7 (paper : alk. paper)
     1. High school teaching—Pennsylvania—Philadelphia. 2. English language—Study and teaching (Secondary)—Pennsylvania—History. 3. African American high school students—Pennsylvania—Philadelphia. 4. Multicultural education—Pennsylvania—Philadelphia. I. Title. II. Series.

LB1607.52.P4F43 2003
373.1102—dc22   2003060204

ISBN 0-8077-4407-7 (paper)
ISBN 0-8077-4408-5 (cloth)

Printed on acid-free paper

Manufactured in the United States of America

11 10 09 08 07 06 05 04   8 7 6 5 4 3 2 1

I dedicate this book to my parents, for never quite understanding me, but accepting the reality of that situation; my daughters, for accepting that understanding me is an ongoing process; and, most of all, my wife, for understanding and accepting me as I am and can be.

Contents

Acknowledgments

In many ways, this entire book is an acknowledgment of the many who have influenced my thinking, writing, and practice across my career. But, specifically, I need to mention a number of people whose input into and support of this book have been invaluable. Shirley Brown, Judy Buchanan, Rachel Ravreby Lintgen, Marsha Pincus, Dina Portnoy, Marci Resnick, and Geoff Winikur have all read and responded to various aspects of this manuscript, and their insights have made for a better book. Sonia Nieto, Jennifer Obidah, and Steve Gordon provided rock solid suggestions in their reviews of the work, along with gentle and kind encouragement. Kathy Schultz, as she did throughout my doctoral work, has lit the way, helping me negotiate the complexities of publication as well as offering great feedback and sound advice.

JoBeth Allen believed in and understood what I was trying to do from the first draft she read and has been instrumental in getting me to stay true to my vision, using equal parts critique and encouragement to do so. Carol Collins has been a patient editor and without that patience I doubt whether the project would have been completed. Susan Lytle and Marilyn Cochran-Smith, as series editors, colleagues, and friends, have also shown amazing patience, and both remain as inspirations to my continued work. Finally, DeAnna Palmer sought permissions, dealt with music publishers, and combed the text on any number of editing missions, all with good humor and efficiency.

To all of these people, I say thank you.

Foreword

Anyone who knows me knows that I am obsessed with context. Although I love theory and am intrigued with method, I am truly obsessed with context. I want to know who, what, where, why, and under what conditions. Thus, as I read, "*Is This English?*" I gravitated to the vivid contextual contours Bob Fecho offers, particularly because of a kinship I share with School District of Philadelphia teachers. Twenty-two years of my life were spent in Philadelphia schools—twelve as a student and ten as a teacher.

I try not to romanticize my Philadelphia experience. It was the hardest work I have ever done. But I also recognize it as a foundation of my understanding of teaching and learning. I also recall that some of the brightest minds were under utilized and unrecognized. I recall that the basketball expression, "come strong or not at all," was a mantra for teaching. Indeed, to have any hope of surviving, one had to work at teaching. I taught in South Philadelphia, North Philadelphia, Germantown, and West Oak Lane. In each of these settings I had my ideas and beliefs challenged. I learned more about the vastness of human capacity, and why humility is perhaps a teacher's most valuable asset.

As Fecho describes the apathy and alienation that characterized his high school, I felt a deep sense of sadness and loss—not just because I remember this high school's glory days, but also because I am so immersed in such loss whenever I go to urban high schools throughout the nation. My own Philadelphia high (where I was a student) suffers from a similar "institutional depression." It is tired, lethargic, angry, apathetic, self-destructive, and locked in a cycle of insignificance, bound to confer upon its students an ever expanding sense of nothingness.

Through what I would describe as a perfect marriage of brilliant storytelling and insightful research, "*Is This English?*" offers the reader an up-close look at the gritty materialism of secondary school teaching with a gossamer overlay of hope. It is gossamer because today's focus on high-stakes testing, zero tolerance, and shape up or ship out policies and procedures make our hope seem almost ethereal—otherworldly and unwise. But Bob Fecho has woven a masterful fabric of hope through his commitment to critical inquiry. This is a book about what it means to care about both whom you teach and what you teach. It is a book about what it means to understand the broader social purposes of schooling and education as possible sites for the advancement of human liberation and the cultivation of democracy. Is this English? Probably. But it is also life.

GLORIA LADSON-BILLINGS

"IS THIS ENGLISH?"

1

A Sense of Beginning; A Beginning of Sense

In 1974, a month after the school year had officially begun, I was hired by the School District of Philadelphia to teach English and reading at Gillespie Junior High School, a monolithic brick edifice in North Philadelphia. I decided to teach in Philadelphia because they had extended an offer of employment and no one else had. I decided to teach at that school because it was near a train and I needed to commute. I decided to teach in the African American community because this neighborhood happened to be predominantly African American. My beginnings as a teacher transacting across culture in classrooms were as simple and as complex as that.

I wish my goals had been loftier than that, that I had been motivated by some altruistic need to help right some inequities in the world and saw teaching in urban schools as a means for doing so. But that wasn't the case. As an Eastern European American and child of the working class, I had managed to get through university by reading and adapting enough of the mainstream culture so as not to call too much attention to myself. I wanted to be a writer, but, married at 18 and emotionally in hock to my parents who had paid for my education, I needed the steady paycheck and benefits package that public school teaching provided. I needed a job. Philadelphia gave me one.

On the day I was hired, Mary Burnett Smith—now a published author of novels, but then the English/reading department chair—took me into her room and had me watch a lesson she taught to a seventh-grade class. As she worked her students through the activities, Mary imbued her lesson with the firm declarations of a woman not to be crossed, at the same time that she individually supported the struggles of her students,

respected their concerns, and praised their triumphs, great and small.
After she was done and the last child had disappeared into the clamor of
the halls, she leveled an eye at me, much in the way I would later see her
do time and again to the students in her charge, and said, "See, Bob,
that's all you have to do. So, you just get up there and teach." She took a
moment to let the words and demonstration sink into my head. "And one
more thing" she said, "You better not be here 2 or 3 years and then run
off to one of those White schools in the Northeast. You'd better stick."

MAKING MEANING

I stuck 24 years—5 at Gillespie with Mary, 3 at University City High School
in West Philadelphia, and 16 at Simon Gratz, the neighborhood high school
that butts against Gillespie. I stuck through two strikes, two layoffs, numerous threatened strikes, and continuously acrimonious labor/management
relations. I stuck through the births of two children, a divorce, and a remar-
riage. I stuck through the terms of four superintendents, eight principals, and
at least nine department heads. I stuck through the joy of seeing hardworking
students graduate, the pain of seeing hardworking students die real or figu-
rative early deaths, the disconcertedness of being called a "muthafucka" by
some students, and the pride of being called friend by others. I stuck through
the looks of worry and concern on the faces of parents, the looks of indifference of too much of the general public, the looks of confidence and accom-
plishment in the eyes of some I taught, and the looks of rage and hopelessness
in the eyes of others I taught. I stuck through the creation of a small learning
community, the establishment of an urban writing project, and the tenuous
embracing of teacher research by some in the educational community. I stuck
through the crushing of a finger that led to an outpouring of concern and
respect, and I stuck through a collaboration of mutual respect that led to a
parting of the ways.

But so what? So do a lot of people—stick, that is—and too often sticking
means that one is just too frightened, too unmotivated, or too something to
get out of the way. I don't think Mary wanted me to just stick, to merely
endure. Instead, she wanted me to stick with a purpose, to find a meaning
for being in these classrooms with these students and working in these ways.

In looking back, I realize that on that first day Mary had started construction on the frame from which I would build outward for the rest of my
educational career. First of all, Mary modeled how teaching is about being
a presence in the classroom, of being a person of substance, of intellectual
weight, of emotional resonance. If I were to help students realize their own
potential, I had to realize my own. Also, teaching is about respect and belief

in my students. I had to see that all students are actors in their environment, with personalities, experiences, and cultures to be valued and built upon for the good of the collective as well as the individual. In addition, teaching is about being there. It is, as I later would say to my student teachers, a marathon and not a sprint. It is about using the inequities of the system not as an excuse for leaving, but as a condition against which you set your purpose every day.

Through Mary's lesson I eventually came to realize that teaching is a slippery paradox—that it was both as easy and simple as she had made it seem that fall morning and as difficult and complex as I would soon discover. All those years ago, she helped me to grasp that teaching is also about what feminist writer Gloria Anzaldua[1] later would call living in the borderlands or educator Mary Louise Pratt[2] would characterize as existing in contact zones. She was helping me to position myself as a teacher of "other people's children" long before sociocultural educator Lisa Delpit[3] would give me language to continue that positioning. By gently, but firmly, guiding me across cultural boundaries on that first day, Mary also opened me to the need to view teaching as a learning experience for which guides, mentors, and networks of support would be invaluable. She was inviting me to read the culture and to find ways to use that reading to help me to gain access.

But perhaps most important for me, Mary helped me to see that teaching and learning were about looking: looking closely, looking over time, looking again, looking with purpose, looking to make sense. Although not in so many words, but by implication, she was saying, "Watch what happens here. There is something to be learned. This is of value." As I sat there watching her, and watching her students, I began to practice tacitly that which eventually I would pry to the surface and use with conscious intent: I was taking an inquiry stance on a classroom, trying to understand from the participants— who now included myself—what it means and what happens when teachers and students inquire into issues of language and literacy across boundaries of race. Trying to increase my understanding of these inquiry transactions became the lens through which I viewed my classroom.

WHAT THIS BOOK IS AND WHAT THIS BOOK ISN'T

So what does it mean to take an inquiry stance? This is a book about that process. Therefore, it is a book about learning through process and about the process of learning. This is a book about learning to teach, about teaching to learn, and about embracing the belief that both activities occur simultaneously throughout one's career. This is a book about the prevalence of questions as well as one about the paucity of answers. This is a book about seeking the truth, yet it is also about never quite finding that truth. This is a book about the search for one true way, all the while knowing there is no one true way. This is a book about trying to get somewhere. This is a book about realizing there is no arriving. This is a book about struggling with paradox. This is a book about understanding that the acceptance of paradox is probably an acceptance of a state of grace. This, obviously, is a book about teaching and learning.

As such, it represents my best effort to make sense of the ways students, parents, student teachers, teacher colleagues, and I came to find meaning in our worlds using literacy as both our topic and our means. By describing my own struggles as I attempted to teach through inquiry and introducing the voices, beliefs, and struggles of some of my students, I give a glimpse—really nothing more is permitted by time and space—into the manner in which inquiry became pervasive within my various teaching situations. Consequently, I describe what that meant for our lives as learners, teachers, and citizens in our flawed, but nevertheless in-process, democracy in the classroom.

Better, Not Best, Practice

Perhaps a better way to understand the purpose of this book is to understand what this book isn't. To start, it is not a book about best practice. I doubt if such a thing exists, despite all the published media and school district rhetoric to the contrary. In my scheme of thinking, there can be no best practice, because there is no reaching such a point. Instead, as teachers, we immerse ourselves in a process of making meaning where we hunker down with our students and constantly seek ways to both connect with them and to help them connect with themselves, one another, and the world around them. Our practice is in constant flux because the world in which we teach is also in constant flux. Therefore, we need a teaching structure on which we can depend, yet still permit improvisation, serendipity, and sway.

S. Leonard Rubenstein, a writing professor I encountered in my undergraduate work at Penn State, used to tell his students that, as writers, we were less than perfect. More to the point, there could be no reaching perfection—that no one in that room, including him, had any hope of becoming the perfect writer. But, he would say with a sly chuckle, we have the rest of our lives to try to approach perfection. That was our hope—a lifetime of honing our skills in search of the unattainable. This absurdity appealed to the existentialist in me, helping me to understand that our lives and all we do with them are in process and it is through the process that we make meaning.

For me, the same existential thinking applies to teaching. In that journey, there is no last step, only a next step. And those steps differ for us all. Even knowing this, I can say there were times I deluded myself into thinking that everyone should teach as I did, that I had this teaching thing pretty squared away. In the early years of the Philadelphia Writing Project (PhilWP), I remember being asked by other teacher consultants to make videos of the teacher/student writing conferences I conducted in my classroom so teachers could use them as a model. As Liz Woods, a fellow TC, and I set out making the videos, I was fairly sure that we were about capturing best practice on that tape. However, this being the mid-1980s, we were both novices with the then relatively new video cams and struggled trying to make showable tapes. This proved fortunate because it forced us to closely examine and repeatedly review the tapes in our possession. What emerged was not best practice. Far from it. Instead, it was practice, alternately filled with insight and rife with flaws. Could it be that I really talked that much in the conference? Why did I let some students take control while I so clearly steered other conferences? What did it mean when I negotiated revision with one student and either ignored or stepped on suggestions of another?

My natural inclination was to destroy those tapes. But through the urging of Susan Lytle and Judy Buchanan, directors of PhilWP at that time, I began to see these tapes in a new light. It wasn't important that these videos were not somebody's best practice; what mattered is that they were somebody's practice, period. Captured on those tapes were teacher/student writing conferences being enacted in a living classroom somewhere in North Philadelphia. Real students with real writing questions were talking with a real teacher. What did my viewing of the tapes mean for my practice? What did others' viewing of the tapes mean for all our practices? What could be learned from those moments on the screen when a conference caught fire and a small epiphany was made? However, perhaps more important, what could be learned when I railroaded a conference to some quick conclusion?

These tapes represented a practice in process, in a continual state of becoming. As an experienced teacher, I knew in my gut that these conferences had changed my classroom. When I stopped standing in front of the class and actually mucked about crablike from desk to desk, as colleague Rayna Goldfarb once described it, I began talking one-to-one with my students. This shift of perspective and transaction changed the atmosphere, the intent, and the ethos of my classroom, as it became more intimate, shared, and personal. I related to students differently and they, consequently, related to me differently. Furthermore, the tapes and the student writing showed this. There was evidence on the screen of connections, eye contact, shared work, shared realizations, and mutual respect. There was evidence on paper that students were writing lengthier, meatier, more cohesive, more creative pieces. However, the screen also showed me dominating some conferences, letting learning moments slip by, or disregarding student cues; the resulting papers showed writing that seemed muddled or formulaic.

As a consequence, I began to rethink the conferences and not throw them away, as I might have earlier in my career. Instead, I looked even more closely at these one-to-one transactions and began to tinker with what occurred when I sat down next to students with the intent of thinking about their work. However, of all ideas gleaned from this looking, perhaps the most important to me was the affirmation that my practice was only at some given place in time and was open to further rethought and a range of possibility. Mine, like that of others, was a practice in process. Eventually, I came to understand that I wasn't searching for a classroom where I did writing conferences; instead I was searching for a classroom where my writing conferences were helping us muck with the texts of our lives in meaningful ways. I had come to see the power of taking what teacher advocates Marilyn Cochran-Smith and Susan Lytle[4] call "a systematic and intentional" look at teaching practice. It was as if I had stepped into a hard-rushing stream and, having been swept away by the current, found myself bubbling to the surface with delight rather than being dragged under.

No Models

So if this is not a book about best practice, it also isn't a book about models. I am proud of many of the lesson plans I have used to support our class inquiries, and the overall scope of the inquiries themselves. I believe the work my students and I did inquiring into issues of the Harlem Renaissance, race and culture in Crown Heights, and life in the working class, represents substantive effort on all our parts and easily could stand as models to replicate. Having said that, I hope that isn't the case. Over 8 years, I inquired into the Harlem Renaissance three times; each time the inquiry had different goals, different purposes, different students, and thus different directions to explore. The end products were different, and both teacher and student ways of working changed. Furthermore, each subsequent inquiry into the Harlem Renaissance was in some way a response to that which had come before. I was taking what I had learned and using it to frame, but not replicate, my efforts. If I were ever to investigate this era again with a class, although there are many elements from previous efforts that I would retain or deepen, there is much that I would do anew.

Therefore, I would be saddened to see exact replicas of my Harlem Renaissance work or any other of the inquiry projects described herein pop up more or less verbatim in classrooms around the country. To have that happen would be missing the point. Such well-intentioned efforts to provide stimulating instruction ignore a key characteristic of an inquiry classroom: Inquiry is grounded in the day-to-day needs of the inquiry group and grows from the particulars of that group. Consequently, no true operating inquiry can resemble another except in the barest frame of essential conditions. Questions need to be raised, evidence needs to be gathered and analyzed, and the researchers need ways to share that which they come to understand. Beyond that, each inquiry has a life, breadth, and character all its own. Therefore, I can imagine many teachers inquiring with their students into issues related to the Harlem Renaissance, but I would hope that those inquiries would be unique to each situation.

In a similar fashion, the classroom is an intersection where theory and practice transact in interesting and complex ways. As teachers, we do our work in a data-rich environment. We evolve a theory of teaching and learning—sometimes purposefully, sometimes tacitly—and bring it to bear upon circumstances that are in constant flux. The work we do with students influences that theory, as do our conversations with colleagues, our readings in the professional literature, and our close observation of the practice in process. Therefore, both theory and practice are embedded in a deep and substantial history that renders them formidable and structurally solid; however, each is also susceptible to the ongoing conversation and is consequently situational and fluid.

The result is that this book is not replete with individual lesson plans of how these inquiries are enacted day to day. I wouldn't reproduce them even if I had them to reproduce. Instead, the intent here is to provide the working theory behind the practice and the working practice behind the theory. The two are in continual dialogue and my intent here is to sketch the frames of these conversations so that others might find a way into the discussion with thoughts of their own. My hope is to help readers to find the reasons, the better to spend their remaining time finding the means for themselves. I respect too much those of us who labor in education, to do otherwise.

Teacher as Learner, Not Crusader

Finally, although large portions of this book deal with my practice in a high school whose student population was 99.5% African American and Caribbean American, this book is not about a White teacher educationally "saving" Black children. Such a concept, so prevalent in mainstream media, is entirely too problematic. First of all, what would I be saving them from? Certainly not their culture. The richness of the working-class Black community was and remains a wonder to me, replete with an honesty, directness, sense of acceptance for those it enfolds, and sense of connectedness to its beliefs. Although some of my students spoke of trying to escape the neighborhood, many spoke of trying to find ways to stay in order to continue to enrich their community. And those who did speak of escape weren't trying to elude their culture; they were tired of the violence and poverty that so much neglect from the mainstream breeds. So if I could, in fact, save students, it would be from the indifference of the mainstream culture that continues to allow such inequity to exist. The political policies that conspire to keep far too many low-income families away from the agency needed to take control of their own situations, are the enemy from which my students needed saving, if such were possible.

But, as I indicated at the start of the chapter, I didn't come into teaching with a messianic call to save. Those who do usually leave the classroom fairly quickly, becoming frustrated in their inability to achieve their goals. However, I did enter teaching to help students realize their own power and potential. At first, that purpose was not always as clear as I would have wanted it, and even as it got more clear, the vision would waver. But as the years slipped past, it became more evident to me. Each of us has the means to generate our own understandings, seek our own sense of meaning, and activate our own agency. But this is not an argument for the rugged individualist and for each of us having the potential to pull ourselves up by our bootstraps. Everything we do is in concert with others, so we also have within us a potential for helping others to realize their own strengths and areas of struggle, as well as their own beliefs and issues. Therefore, to teach is to provide a framework upon which other individuals can outwardly build their own frameworks for learning. It wasn't about saving students; it was about saving time and opportunity to assist students toward self-actualization and self-empowerment.

If this book is about anyone being saved, then it is my own salvation as a teacher—largely achieved through teaching in the Black community—that must be noted. I am a shy and reserved person by nature and nurture, and feel that if I had started teaching in a middle-class mainstream community, I most likely would have remained so. Such culture tends to reward the quiet side of me. However, my students and their families brought me face to face— sometimes in my face—with a directness and exuberance of emotion that I rarely had seen in my own education. When they liked me, they told me in big ways, and when they were angry, I got the same largeness of response. When invited to party with the families of students, I saw the flamboyant nature of celebration. When allowed into circles of grief, I witnessed deep pain expressed without reserve or shame. Whether being reviled because of what being a White male represented to students who hadn't come to know me as a person, or being embraced with a depth of trust by those who had, a full range of emotion was always possible, always expected, and, eventually, always appreciated.

All of this gave me permission to explore ways of living larger in the classroom, of developing the persona and presence Mary Smith alluded to on our first meeting. To this day, no one could describe me as flamboyant and extremely outgoing. Yet, I also know that I would not even have attempted this book if I hadn't learned how to project a larger image of myself through my involvement of 24 years teaching in the Black community.

Locally Focused; Globally Implied

Finally, although much of this book is about the crossing of cultures in classrooms, the implications are not limited only to educators seeking to understand pedagogies that embrace diversity. Much of my work took place in an urban, secondary classroom, but the implications can be understood and made relevant by teachers in other sites that do not share those characteristics. I will be among the first to profess that place and context matter, that a classroom of working-class White students in rural Georgia differs markedly from a multicultural classroom in urban San Francisco. However, I also believe that relevance, like meaning, lies in the transaction between reader and text. This book informs educators about the way working-class Black students construct meaning; yet I suspect and hope that all us who labor among schoolchildren, no matter what their cultural background, can find meaning for themselves in these pages. What went on in my classroom has import for all classrooms. Therefore, I hold it imperative to see the ideas discussed here as relevant to all learners who endeavor to read the word and the world, as revolutionary educator Paulo Freire[5] suggests.

BUILDING A FRAMEWORK

The framework of this book builds upon some fairly supple structures. It is about what literary theorist Louise Rosenblatt[6] has called transactions, the way we shape and are shaped by texts we encounter. In particular, it looks closely at the way inquiry transactions in the classroom—how we raise and investigate questions that arise from a range of texts—help us to use our literacy to develop meaning and use our inquiry to develop our literacy. The book asks what it means to take an inquiry stance on a critical inquiry classroom. The understandings resulting from various investigations into threads of that larger question are the stuff of these chapters.

The classroom in question is mine; this is a form of practitioner research. Most of the artifacts for this study were collected from 1990 to 1998 in a galaxy far, far away. Or so it seems, now that I teach and research my practice at the University of Georgia. That galaxy was Simon Gratz High School, about which more description will be forthcoming in later chapters. But by reading and thinking about artifacts from this time and space, as well as asking others to read and think about those artifacts, I have constructed an overlapping composite of what it meant to inquire with colleagues and students into issues of substance. Those artifacts—collected student work; transcriptions of audio- and videotaped class sessions; transcriptions of individual and group interviews; dialogue journals between me and a student teacher; collected student evaluations, reflections, and reaction sheets; a form of notes about events in class dictated as they occurred or shortly thereafter into a hand-held cassette; and a range of reconstructed vignettes—seem simultaneously more than enough and hopelessly incomplete for the task at hand. As seems to be the case for many of us who document our practice, at times I was facile in my ability to collect data and at other times I would wonder why so much time had passed and I had collected so little. Frequently the deciding factor between these times would be how much my students needed me to be a teacher and not a researcher.

This book explains the way I transacted in my classroom—with my students, colleagues, the larger community of my school, and the larger educational community of theorists and researchers. It makes a case for understanding education, both in and out of schools, as a series of transactions that allow us to deepen and expand our understanding of the world and ourselves in relation to that world. It shows how, by taking an inquiry stance on my classroom, I enabled myself and my students to transact in ways that gave us options and possibilities rather than dictates and fatalities. In doing so, it shows our struggles, our missteps, and our conflicts, as it also shows our evolution, grace, and collaborative understanding. This book is about teacher as learner and learner as teacher and what it means to call all classroom perspectives into question.

In her book, *Children's Inquiry*, Judith Lindfors[7] debunks one myth about the relationship between questions and competency in a subject matter. She notes that frequently we expect the novice to have not only many questions, but interesting, thought-provoking questions to boot. Lindfors maintains that the majority of people, when embarking on a journey of inquiry, have only general questions with which to start. Mostly they want to know, "What is such and such?" or, "How do I do such and such?" It is only through concerted inquiry over time that most people are able to develop questions that push their thinking and that of others in more complicated and sophisticated ways. It is a Zen-like notion that the more we know, the more able we are to articulate what we don't know and to ask questions that will redirect our inquiry in ever-more focused ways.

This book is one attempt on my part, in a process that has been developing for over 15 years, to rethink my questions and thus to make new meaning of a range of individual inquiries. In essence, I want to ask better questions, ones that will build on my understandings to date and open new avenues of thought for me and those with whom I come into contact. The hope is to discuss the ways my theory and practice have transacted over this time span and to help me understand what this might mean for my own pedagogy and that of others endeavoring to implement what I call critical inquiry pedagogy. Perhaps more important, I hope this focused reflection yields an agenda of questions that will help all of us interested in these ideas to further our understandings with renewed effort and greater result.

2

Hopelessness and Possibility

That early spring day in 1989, my last-period class came in as they usually did, chatty, bubbly, full of life. My experience with last-period classes is that it was all you could do to keep them from slipping out the door when you weren't looking. Usually everyone, including the teacher, is consumed by the crawl of the clock that, due to a corollary of the law of watched pots, moves even slower than normal. Lessons that spring to life in other periods often die an anguished death in the last one of the day.

But that wasn't the case with this particular class. Fueled by an inquisitive core of young women, these juniors were usually ready to muck with literature, with language, and with literacy. We had spent two-thirds of a school year engaging in discussions, conferences, revisions, and final products. Through all our hard struggles together, we had evolved an ease of relationship. They were a group I could laugh, relax, and share more of myself with.

So, when I offered Nikki Giovanni's "Beautiful Black Men" to that group, I was at once absolutely prepared for and totally unsuspecting of what happened next. Although its lines contain such dated terms as "outasite Afros" and "driving their hogs," I saw the poem as a celebration of African American identity in straightforward street language and dialect. It was, I thought, safe—meaning that it seemed to have no political edge relative to other poems by the author—and would stir no controversy in my class. After all, the season was, as e. e. cummings tells us, "just spring." The sun was slicing through the pinholes and slashes in our window shades and what breeze we could muster from the alley between two schools promised warmer days ahead. This was to be a romp through some celebratory literature. My purpose for studying this poem was to examine the vivid and colloquial use of language by Giovanni and to perhaps use it as a springboard for student generation of poetry that reflected their own pride in their culture. Nothing grander or less significant than that.

Yet, as the class finished the group reading, I could see that they were unsettled. There was a terseness about their responses to my questions that was quite unlike their usual affability. Through the year they had challenged, teased, and questioned me, but rarely shut me out. However, this poem, which I thought would set them talking about life "back in the day" and the positive African American images inherent within the verse, instead had made them tight-lipped and seemingly disgruntled. Moreover, when I mentioned their disquietude, their response was that it was really nothing and I shouldn't worry. Rather than energetically talking about positive issues of culture or, at the very least, laughing at how quickly slang dates itself, the class instead had stilled their voices to mumbles that I struggled to discern.

Perhaps, prior to that moment, I would have let it drop, ignored the awkwardness as I had done in the past, and gone on to the next poem. But I didn't—couldn't—and I pressed the issue. Finally Latonya, who was always upfront about her opinions, blurted, "She making fun of the way Black people talk."

There it was. Out on the floor. I thought the poem to be a celebration. I believed Nikki Giovanni intended it as such. But my students saw it as a put down, a parody. We could either sit and stare open-mouthed at the gap in our perspectives or we could summon up the courage to ask the next question. My students had run smack against a problem of language, and a seemingly innocent poem had left them bewildered, angry, and betrayed. Some were upset with me because I had chosen this poem that seemed to belittle their race and consequently themselves. Others were angry at Giovanni who they first supposed to be White and then, upon learning she was of their race, grew angrier at her betrayal. Finally, others expressed the concern that their neighbors and classmates, through the omnipresent use of dialect and slang, made themselves such easy targets for parody. My "safe" poem had heated up in ways both political and personal. And life in my classroom would never be the same.

MAKING MEANING

I have long believed that one reason teachers drag themselves home exhausted is because they are the lids that sit upon the emotional, intellectual, and physical pressure cookers we more commonly call classrooms. In teaching spaces, things happen. No matter what amount of control, consistency, and management is offered, things happen. And that's as it should be. I don't want to teach with every moment planned out and every response predictable. On the other hand, having to contend with all the possibility of a classroom, the attention that must be paid, is wearying to the bone. A teacher with a hearing impairment said that she went home exhausted from my university class because all the collaborative work forced her to concentrate so hard in order to hear everything. I told her I could relate because, as someone whose job I felt it was to attend to all those threads and eventualities, I too was exhausted for the same reasons.

The Giovanni poem vignette is a good example of a class lesson taking on a life of its own, one that wasn't anticipated, but, like a well-written mystery, seems evident in retrospection. It is what I have come to see as a teachable, researchable moment. For a slim minute, that class was perched on a fulcrum, waiting for our cumulative weight to carry us toward or away from the questions that were raised. Particularly at that point in my teaching, although there was only one of me, my decision toward or away probably would have swayed the group. Their reluctance to talk was already in evidence. All I had to do was decide it was time to move on and that probably would have been that.

However, questions had been raised and the raising of those questions had made something buzz in the classroom that the unseasonably warm temperatures couldn't explain in and of themselves. My students had gone beyond a mere informational reading of the poem and, instead, were displaying strong emotional reactions. What was even more intriguing was that one of my intentions prior to reading the poem was to trigger such a response. It's just that my anticipated love-in for this lyric from the 1960s became, instead, a spontaneous protest.

To my everlasting good fortune, I decided that I couldn't flinch from the questions being raised, nor could my students. I had arrived at a juncture in my teaching that positively demanded that I pay attention and commit to either preserving the status quo or rethinking my classroom. How I responded to this moment will be described in the rest of the book. However, some of how I came to this juncture and subsequent rethinking of my teaching, is the stuff of this chapter.

THE SETTING: APATHY AND ALIENATION

My sense of Simon Gratz High School in the 1980s, having arrived in 1982, was different from that of many of the teachers who had been teaching there from the 1970s. To them, the school had seen better days, but still retained a sense of tradition and purpose. They particularly remember when Marcus Foster—who later would become superintendent of the Oakland, California, schools only to be assassinated by the Symbionese Liberation Army—had been principal. There, in the turbulent 1960s, the staff had banded together with the community to deal with a student population well over 3,000, a school on a double-shift schedule to accommodate those numbers, and a rising gang problem. Life may have been tumultuous, but it also was deeply embedded in the Black Pride movement, and many graduates at that time went on to play leadership roles in the Philadelphia community. Some became teachers and eventually found their way back to Simon Gratz as faculty members. They spoke of the band marching down Hunting Park Avenue before football games, of the many after-school clubs and activities, of political activism, and of the wide and varied sports offerings anchored by wrestling and basketball.

By the time I arrived at Simon Gratz, there was no band. Most of what they spoke of no longer existed. True, the school was and remains a basketball power in the public league, but in 1985, if the last bell rang at 2:10 in the afternoon, by 2:15 you could throw an eraser down any hallway and have little fear of hitting anyone. There were few traditional activities taking place with any periodic regularity that one associates with most flourishing high schools. One physics class served a school of 2,000 students, and the foreign language department consisted of one full- and one half-time teacher. Along with the band, the majority of the clubs and service activities also disappeared. The lunchroom situation become so chaotic that the decision was made to dismantle the cafeteria and have all students dismissed for lunch as their last scheduled period.

What few programs did exist, received little support and managed to survive mainly through the efforts of dedicated individuals. An enduring image for me is the sight of Deidre Farmbry—the newspaper faculty sponsor at that time who was to eventually become Chief Academic Officer for the school district—selling candy between class periods in order to meet basic printing costs. With little to keep them there, too many students and faculty competed with each other for quick egress when the dismissal bell rang.

My overall sense was one of apathy and alienation. Given reduced resources, the school leadership and staff struggled to maintain a shrinking status quo. Whatever was left of the proud tradition of Simon Gratz remained in the memories of those who had experienced it and was not made manifest in the day-to-day actions of the school. Therefore, I didn't see it, nor did the student body, most of whom couldn't find ways to leave school fast enough. Not that they were doing anything more exciting or of greater import. Very often, students would cut class only to cluster about on the corners and curbs outside the school. Those who elected to remain often received less attention than they needed and deserved, due to the randomness of scheduling and the sheer work load of teachers handling five classes of 33 students spread across six periods. In some ways at that time, Gratz didn't even fit the classic stereotype of an inner-city school, of a place beset with drugs, violence, and classroom disruption. For too many students, the school had become such a nonentity in their lives that even such overt signs of resistance seemed not worth the effort.

The morale among many staff members was not much better. Forced desegregation of faculty in the late 1970s had sent strong and young Black role models to predominantly White schools in the city, to be replaced with White teachers, many of whom resented the new assignment. In addition, voluntary student desegregation caused the creation of magnet high schools around the city, drawing financial, human, and political resources away from comprehensive neighborhood high schools like Simon Gratz. Working in schools drained of multiple layers of support, young leadership, and a larger core of students who had a history of academic success, too many staff members simply bided their time until a transfer to a "better"—code for White or academic—school came through. I find it emblematic that, when central administration offered me the right to return to my previous high school assignment and I elected to remain at Simon Gratz, the principal announced my choice in faculty meetings on two separate occasions. Her point was that my electing to stay was evidence that Simon Gratz wasn't so bad. Although I appreciated being valued, I somehow felt that if conditions had been strong at the school, one new teacher's comings or goings wouldn't have merited such fanfare.

As I looked into the educational literature of that time, it became evident that the sense of alienation and apathy I was witnessing at Simon Gratz was not restricted to that school. Studies of urban adolescents in educational settings drew a picture of a student population at odds with its surroundings. Those who elected to stay stumbled through schools where boredom reigned, where belief in the system of education was low, and where even so-called "good" students hid their skills in order to gain acceptance into adolescent culture.[1] As sociocultural researcher Jean Anyon[2] pointed out, the curriculum and pedagogy for schools of most marginalized populations was one of domesticity. The work of school was deadening, intended to prepare students for the even more deadening factory work and service jobs that awaited them. And those who elected to leave, often did so for reasons other than because they couldn't keep up academically. Instead, according to social psychologist Michelle Fine,[3] they had found school to be a disinviting and frequently hostile place that often silenced their voices and offered no challenging and relevant curriculum, nor did much to discourage their departure.

As I looked at Simon Gratz as it shifted toward the 1990s, the signs of alienation and apathy described in the academic literature were prevalent.

Most students seemed disaffected from their courses and even those who endeavored to at least play along wanted to do so under a minimum of expectations. For their part, the staff was largely conscientious, but too frequently drew their line of engagement far too short. Those of us who wanted more seemed powerless to effect much change beyond the walls of our individual classrooms. I found myself wondering if it would be better to cut my losses and move on to some other line of work.

WHAT COUNTS AS LEARNING

As I tried to cope with my own growing sense of powerlessness in terms of affecting change in the larger school, I concentrated more and more on trying to change what took place in my classroom. Even though I was somewhat restricted by 50-minute periods and a system of scheduling that dropped students into slots in a fairly random array, I kept trying to evolve my teaching in ways that more deeply engaged students. The effort to do various forms of teacher/student conferencing was an indication of this, as was a greater willingness on my part to diverge more and more from the canon. My whole intent was to develop a curriculum that felt seamless. I wanted sessions that flowed from writing to reading to speaking to language study and back in a cohesive and meaningful loop.

Vocabulary, however, always seemed to stick in my curricular craw. Few activities seemed more ingrained in the traditional English class than the weekly vocabulary and spelling test. Whether the words were generated from stories or pulled off published lists, the weekly quiz and eventual review test appeared ubiquitous. I found this particularly nettlesome for several reasons. First of all, an enormous amount of time was spent memorizing lists, but I rarely saw the words emerge in student language and speech. In addition, even recognition retention seemed to fade quickly after the assessment. Also, some students were maintaining fairly high averages because they memorized well and consequently scored well on the quizzes. Yet, as readers and writers, these same students struggled in ways that indicated that they were less secure in their language use than the quizzes were indicating. In my heart, I had no great love for this way of learning vocabulary, but couldn't seem to eliminate it from my program. The weight of tradition and conventional wisdom about SATs loomed large.

This all came to a head one day when a student looked at me and said, "Wow, I'm smart." Too curious to let that declaration pass, I asked why she felt that way. "I'm smart because I always get an A on my vocabulary quiz. That shows I'm really thinking." I smiled and tried to validate her hard won sense of pride, but couldn't help feeling that something was out of synch.

This student was sharp and insightful, but my evidence for that wasn't these quizzes. Instead, I based my assertion on her ability to make sense of complicated text, to express herself through writing and speech in complicated ways, and to react to complicated classroom situations with thought and insight. To her, thinking and intelligence were equated with memorization fostered by rote drill. She had learned this message in other classrooms, but I was certainly helping her to reify the belief that to memorize and regurgitate was to think in sophisticated ways.

This vignette illustrates how the ways we teach and assess speak volumes about what counts as learning and demonstrations of that learning. As Freire has noted, much of what counts for learning in public schools could be described as a "banking model" of education, one in which students are mere repositories for information dumped there by teachers. This student showed strong ability to use literacy in her life, but evidence for me lay in those activities that encouraged her to make meaning of that which she read in the world. For her, the evidence lay in her ability to parrot words, although she probably would not describe it as such. At any rate, one can't blame her because probably the most frequent and consistent way in which she was asked to demonstrate the extent of her learning and for which rewards were equally frequent and consistent were multiple-choice or short-answer assessments of this type.

Prompted by this vocabulary discussion and similar incidents, I delved into educational literature that described high school curriculums that demanded little in the way of thinking from students.[4] As educator Grant Wiggins[5] noted, the emphasis was on coverage—getting through all the material in the book—rather than creating deep structures of learning—having the material "get through" to the student in substantive and enduring ways. To counter this trend, I continued evolving a way to teach that would expect more of students. I remember frequently saying, almost chanting to students, that becoming a scrivener was no longer a job option, that copiers could reproduce the written page far faster and with greater fidelity than we humans could. The mere reproduction of information, if it ever had been a worthwhile aim of education, certainly no longer seemed useful, timely, or rewarding. Instead, we needed to experience learning that required us to analyze, synthesize, categorize, and otherwise process or make sense of information. We could not count ourselves learners and theorizers otherwise.

RACE, LANGUAGE, AND CULTURE

My experience with the Giovanni poem led me to consider issues of race and language in very different ways than I previously had. It's not that race issues were nonexistent in my classroom. I am an Eastern European American male who was then teaching classes composed solely of Black students, largely African Americans with some Caribbean Americans. Race had to enter my practice. There was no denying racial factors and the manner in which these factors both enabled and complicated the way I taught. African American authors were always a staple of my literature selection and I made increasingly more deliberate efforts to learn from my students that which I could not know for myself—what it meant to grow up Black in White America. In addition, in coping with issues of dialect, I had for some time tried to provide situations that allowed my students to operate in the classroom in both home and power codes—the languages, values, and conventions of their families and of the mainstream, respectively.[6]

Yet so many of my early forays across cultural boundaries were what I would characterize as being either too subtle or too safe. Like many White teachers in Black schools, I didn't quite know what to do with my privilege and my relative isolation. The former caused a certain amount of guilt, and the latter a certain amount of trepidation. Having discussions about race in which I was frequently the sole White present usually meant stumbling through both this guilt concerning White attitudes about Blacks, and these worries that I might somehow offend or misrepresent; neither emotional journey was something I enjoyed. Another continual concern was that some question at some point was going to put me on a spot from which I couldn't retreat, and some unexamined bias on my part would be revealed. Too often the issues seemed much easier to touch on rather than to engage with any depth.

Compounding these feelings was the fact that, in somewhat of a role reversal, I often was now viewed as a spokesperson for my race. If classroom situations ventured across cultural boundaries, my students frequently expected my opinion to count for that of all Whites. I remember seventh-grade students pulling a tendril of my then longer hair and unnerving me with both the tactile connection and the question: Do all White people have hair as straight as this? If we were reading a poem such as Countee Cullen's "Incident" in which a Black child experiences what generally is perceived as his first blatant act of racist aggression, students would query me about the psyche of Whites who would do such a thing, the very mind-set from which I was laboring to distance myself. Even though I knew I could not represent the views of or apologize for the actions of all Whites, sensing that many students expected this of me added a burden to my interaction.

Therefore, to somewhat buffer myself at these border crossings, I would try to downplay the very racial issues I was opening to scrutiny via my choice of literature or expression of subject matter for discussion. We would read the works of Langston Hughes or Alice Walker, but these readings were too regularly embedded in a phalanx of other, more mainstream works. Discussions frequently were framed to touch on issues of race, but also limited in ways that would leave our interrogation bobbing mostly on the surface of complexity's sea. Feeding all this was the fact that my literature choices usually reflected the most anthologized and accessible Black authors. This often meant that students encountered a fairly narrow band of African American literature and that which tended to touch on universal themes rather than those more particular to race and racism. I can't say I did all of this consciously, but, in retrospect, it seems all too evident. I was trying to bring race and race issues into my classroom, but kept doing it in ways that caused my efforts to be less than what I wanted in terms of impact. What I was doing was better than avoiding the subject entirely, but I was selling us all short in terms of expecting what we could handle and learn together about race.

REASONS FOR BEING

As if being unnerved by issues of race and language weren't enough, I also found myself wondering about the purpose of education in the first place. My working-class roots had ingrained two key, if somewhat contrary, axioms into my central nervous system. The first was that I needed to be proud of where I came from. The second was that one sure way to enable me to leave where I came from was through education. In subtle and not so subtle ways, my parents hammered those two somewhat competing ideas home. Don't forget where you came from, they urged, but make sure to use education to put you into a social position where you at least might be tempted to forget where you came from. Learning out of school—acquiring common sense—was a means for functioning in the neighborhood. Learning in school was seen as a means for advancing one's social status and bettering one's economic conditions. It also meant, at least to me, having to use a form of the impersonal pronoun *one*, as I did in the previous sentence, as opposed to the more personal use of the second person *you*, as I did in an earlier sentence. If the goals were economic and social advancement, the price was personal change and a certain degree of acceptance of or fluency in the language and systems of the middle class.

Most of my students came from families where the parents toiled in industrial or service positions, if such jobs were available. If possible, both parents worked, often odd hours that frequently caused them to be away from home when school was over. Of necessity, many of my students had become very adept at taking care of their own needs after school, as well as those of younger siblings. Therefore, on the surface at least, the students I taught seemed very open to economic arguments for education.

This appeared to be so much the case that I often would have discussions that I labeled as "Saying the Litany." At some point, I would ask students why they were in school. The immediate response would be, "To get an education." I would then ask, "Why do you want an education?" to which they would answer "To get a job." Finally, I would ask the purpose of the job. "To make lots of money," or some variation thereof would be the reply. Like a litany, the whole exchange had an almost chant-like rhythm to it, and I suspect if I had been raised in a Black Baptist or Pentecostal church rather than Catholic, I might have labeled this call and response. Whatever the label, year after year, class after class, I could trot out these questions and expect little variance in terms of answers.

However, I am a lapsed Catholic, and one reason I cite for this disenchantment is that saying the litany for me was just that—saying words I had memorized, but not embraced. It had become a recitation of duty or expectation rather than an utterance of depth and meaning. I said the words of the litany, but I didn't feel them.

I began to suspect the same of my students as they told me why they came to school. If school were important to them and if it translated into social and economic advancement, then why did so many seem to go out of their way not to fully engage in the work of school? Given readings and writings to do at home, many would either opt out of the assignment or turn in a half-hearted effort. If given a task to complete in class, many students would open the book, but then never turn a page or move a pen across a line. Too often, students had to be hounded to take the SATs and walked through the college application procedure. Why did getting by seem to be the goal, rather than excelling?

As I listened more to my students, I began to hear answers similar to those educational anthropologist John Ogbu[7] described in his work. In essence, although a good deal of verbal attention was paid to the importance of school in the working-class Black community to which I was connected, actual belief in school's power to alter economic and social conditions for large numbers of Blacks had been eroded by too much anecdotal evidence to the contrary. From my perspective, it's not so much that the students and their families had lost complete belief in the power of education; after all, many students continued to show up day after day. In fact, education was deeply valued in the families of the students I taught. It was school and the mainstream power structure that weren't trusted. Their reaction was more agnostic than educational-neutral. Most wouldn't *not* believe, but, until they saw more hard proof to the contrary, they weren't about to go on blind faith alone. Given the racist track record of the United States, who could blame them for questioning the litany rather than embracing it?

And hard proof in support of schooling was hard to come by. My students could see men and women in their neighborhood with high school and even college degrees, whose social and economic status had been altered little by their hard work and deep investment in personal initiative. The harsh realities of racist policies and subtexts in the United States had created a situation where more and more Blacks were completing higher and higher levels of education, but the circumstances of the inner city remained the same. A Black from North Philadelphia with a high school or even college degree was not in the same position to exploit that degree as a White with the same credentials living in the Philadelphia suburbs.

This left me with somewhat of a crisis in my classroom. If both my students and I had doubts about the economic arguments for embracing education as it traditionally was offered in schools, what reason could I put forth for taking all this time out of their lives? When I was honest with myself, I knew that my continual search as a lifelong learner was about that search and not the material and societal perks that might accompany it. For my students, the implications were more dire and immediate. If they could, at the age of 16 or younger, enter the illegal economy that operated in their neighborhoods and make substantially more money and do it faster with a greater guarantee of return of investment than a high school graduate, what could I offer as a reason for learning in academic ways? I remember one Gratz graduating class from the mid-1980s that selected "It's all over now" as their class motto. If this were true—if high school commencement really wasn't a new beginning, but some form of societal and academic euthanasia—what was my counterproposal? If belief in the words were eroded by the realities of the situation, what good was the litany?

FLASHES OF BRILLIANCE

I remember reading Patrick Shannon's *The Struggle to Continue: Progressive Reading Instruction in the United States*[8] and shaking my head in frustration. I know this was not the reaction he intended for readers. As he states in his preface, his hope was for his book to describe "the century-long struggle to continue [progressive literacy education] well enough to encourage more and more teachers to continue to struggle in order to realize the connection between literacy and what John Dewey called 'true democracy.'"[9] Yet as I finished reading Shannon's words, I couldn't help feeling like throwing in the towel. What was the point, I thought. If John Dewey and so many other committed educators couldn't make the concepts of progressive literacy education stick in the political, social, and educational consciousness of mainstream America, what were my chances of pulling it off in my small corner of the educational world, especially in the face of such public indifference?

Several factors intervened somewhat sequentially within a time span of 5 years to mitigate my second great lapse of faith: I was accepted into the inaugural summer institute of PhilWP, I initiated graduate studies at the University of Pennsylvania, and efforts were started to reform comprehensive high schools using funding from the Pew Trust funneled through the Philadelphia Schools Collaborative. Yet, as key and as empowering as these experiences were—and more will be said about the influence of each in the next chapter—I doubt if they could have shaken me from a growing sense of hopelessness, if one other factor hadn't been occurring all through my career. Despite the overt signs of apathy and more covert doubt regarding the effectiveness of education as a transforming element in their lives, a wide range of students, on a daily basis, displayed what can only be described as flashes of brilliance.

These insights into their potential were shown in a variety of ways: a seemingly disinterested student would connect with a certain story or poem and come alive; the intermittent attendee with the gruff attitude unexpectedly would soften and become a linchpin of the class; a hard worker suddenly would grasp an idea at a deeper level and burst aglow in pride; the bland writer of essays would erupt into a grand writer of plays or the reverse might come true; the student who never uttered a word to the large group would summon up enough courage and support to complete a presentation to the whole class.

Two stories will serve as examples of all the tales I could tell here, but for which I haven't the room. Marquita was assigned to my class, but well into September, she still hadn't shown up. Anyone teaching in an urban school knows that such cases frequently result when students transfer; the system is slow to pick up the paper trail. But Marquita remained on my rolls, so I contacted her home trying to find out the problem. The next day an obviously angry Marquita showed up, but resolutely declined to do any work. I approached her afterward to try to get at her concerns. "You was the one who called my house? What's it your business, what I do with my life." She almost spat the words at me. "Wait a minute," I responded. "Let me get this straight. I call your home because I care about what happens to you, that you get something from your education, that you use your learning to make a place for yourself in life. I do this for you and you get angry at me?" There was a stunned silence for a moment before she shrugged her shoulders and left.

But she showed up the next day and participated in class. As the weeks went by, she became more and more involved in the work and showed a particular flair for classroom discussion and writing. In my class, all the gruff exterior that Marquita showed to most of the world melted, revealing a polite and sincere young woman with a gift for learning. In particular, she would use the literature in class as starting points for papers about the way her life connected to the stories.

But one day, she was absent, and then two, and then a week. When I inquired I found out that a family relative who had been in jail for abusing her and others had come back into her neighborhood and she had gone off to live with distant relatives. Like a fall leaf, she had blazed quickly and then fallen away. But how brilliant the color for that time.

On the other hand, G-Man had come to stay. Affable and gregarious, G-Man intended to graduate as long as it didn't cost him too much effort. He was smart enough to know that if he went to all his classes and did all his work, he could reach his goal and really not have to break an intellectual sweat. He was hard not to like and I did like him, but my hope was that he would discover more of a purpose for his education than just getting through.

It took about half a year, but the one-to-one engagement of our writing conferences provided the jumpstart he needed. Grasping that these conferences gave him second chances and insight into his process, G-Man began to take class seriously. He embraced the idea of revision and eagerly used our conferences to learn about his writing. First drafts soon were of better quality than final copies from earlier in the year. His ability to sustain both discussion and interest developed and he soon became a class leader; others came to expect him to weigh in on issues. When he graduated, he did so with a greater sense of satisfaction for having come to appreciate the value of concerted academic work.

There are no miracles in these stories, and others, that my colleagues and I could tell—just hard work connected to talents that would emerge when given proper circumstances, and small flashes of intellectual fire that sustained our hope even as our grasp of the absurd helped us to cope with the cruelties of the system. As the ninth decade of the twentieth century came to a close, we were witnessing what Lisa Delpit[10] later would more explicitly urge all teachers who teach across cultural boundaries to seek.

> Teachers must not merely take courses that tell them how to treat their students as multicultural clients. . . . They must also learn about the brilliance the students bring with them "in their blood." Until they appreciate the wonders of the culture represented before them . . . they cannot appreciate the potential of those who sit before them, nor can they link their students' histories and worlds to the subject matter they present in the classroom.

At least I was getting the first part of that admonition: I was seeing the brilliance and appreciating the wonders of the culture. Making the needed links was more difficult. But there were days when more of such linking happened.

These tentative connections seemed to then make other connections appear possible. But what eluded me too often at mid-career was putting enough of those good days together in succession. I needed my teaching to mesh strong theory with strong practice, needed to be a strong teacher with strong students and supported by strong colleagues. That was my question—how to pull off such teaching?

3

Two's Company; Three's a Small Learning Community

I stood propped against the frame of my classroom doorway as a kind of choreographed chaos swept around me. We were between bells and the halls were filled with chatter of gossip, rifts of rap, and the occasional profanity as students showed no outward signs of hurry to get to their next class. My presence there served to give the overzealous student pause, entering students a sense of welcome, and timid students a sense of security. I could even take the moment to conference over some small concern with a student I had caught en route.

This afternoon as I stood there, Marsha Pincus walked over from her room next door. Marsha, along with Natalie Hiller and me, had co-founded Crossroads, our small learning community (SLC) or school within a school. Together, Marsha and I were the English department for our SLC. A teacher researcher in her own right, a strong advocate for student voice, and someone who used playwriting as a means to stimulate students' exploration of their own lives, Marsha loved to discuss educational issues, whether at an SLC meeting, standing in the gray cold of our school parking lot, or, as in this case, in the 5 minutes between classes. In even this short time, our topics of conversation were rarely the minutiae of teaching one finds in faculty rooms—what the last announcement was about, where the faculty meeting is. Instead we frequently would raise issues of pedagogy and theory as we stood in the midst of this swirl of action. It's amazing how deep ideas can go in 5 minutes' dialogue.

This day was no different. Marsha had in hand a draft of a piece I was writing about a former student of mine and how that student saw herself in terms of language and race. I had given it to Marsha for feedback, not only because she knew both the student and the circumstances surrounding our work, but because she brought great insight to such things and I could always count on a critical, but fair, reading.

Despite the bustle of the hall, she managed to click off a few salient points about what she liked and what could be improved. Her task done and the late bell ringing, Marsha started to move toward her classroom as I hurried some lingering students through my doorway. However, she paused and added, "I can see why you hated to lose Laura."

These words instantly grabbed my attention, less for the fact that she knew I missed Laura now that Laura had graduated, then because I was curious as to what connection Marsha had made. She has an amazingly associative mind and some of her best ideas are given in loosely connected afterthoughts.

"Laura for you," she continued, "was like Jeremy and Malisha for me. Laura pushed your thinking. She challenged you. Her thoughts were complex and not easy."

I mumbled some agreeing response and thanked Marsha for this and her other comments. Although she rushed back to start her class, I stood at my door, despite the rising roar within. Marsha's words were running through my head: "Laura pushed your thinking. She challenged you."

As I swung the door of my classroom closed, I realized that my piece needed to be not just about Laura and her issues around language and race, but about how my perspective on these issues transacted with what she brought. This work was about the two of us and what we said to each other and how what we said shaped us in the saying. I resolved to write my piece about Laura and me as a window into not just her mind, but mine as well.

MAKING MEANING

I've often wished that I had documented these hallway sessions and the myriad other talks Marsha and I had in our years teaching together. These discussions with her, Natalie, and any number of my colleagues from Crossroads formed a basis for an ongoing professional development, one that we owned and that always emanated from our essential needs as classroom teachers. The stuff of these discussions invariably found its way into our practice and our reflections on that practice to once again emerge in some later musing about why and how we did what we did in classrooms.

Like most texts, this vignette leaves itself open for multiple interpretations. For my purposes here, however, it gives insight into the ways transactions with colleagues, as well as those with students, push teachers to make deeper and more connective sense of practice. This point is particularly true if these transactions take the form of inquiries. As Judith Lindfors[1] suggests, not all questions are inquiries and not all inquiries are questions. In this case with Marsha, an inquiry was initiated on her part, even though all her ideas were delivered as statements. But what is difficult to replicate on the printed page is her tone and her timing. She was thinking about these thoughts even as she gave them voice, rethinking how her own students transacted in important ways with her. Furthermore, her words were nudging me to reconsider my own work and to see how Laura and I were transacting around these issues.

It is through such inquiries, informal and of the moment, that teaching evolves, at least on a daily basis. However, networking with colleagues also can be more formal and less immediate. This chapter traces the ways I entered into dialogue with colleagues via a range of teacher networks.

SKEINS OF UNDERSTANDING

I taught for 8 years next to Marsha Pincus. During that time, our voiced educational philosophy was so in concert that we usually could finish one another's sentences. Yet, student teachers whose supervision we shared would remark about how different our classrooms were in tone, physical setup, and focus. That we would enact a common philosophy in different ways gives me hope that educators reading the discussion here will be able to transact with the ideas, but still implement those ideas in ways that complement the culture of their own classrooms. And I like to think that, on most points of educational substance, Marsha and I can still finish one another's sentences.

But it was Marsha who first raised for the both of us the importance of what she called "embracing the dissonance."[2] What she was referring to was the need for teachers to look closely and systematically at whatever in their classrooms seemed out of synch, grounded in struggle, or counter to expectations. Too frequently, we and other teachers would either dismiss such departures from our norms as anomalies or simply ignore or abandon the problems. With so much to do, it seemed easier to move on rather than touch upon issues that appeared too tender to touch. However, not to look with deliberation and intent meant, too often, not to grow as both teachers and learners. Marsha, I, and many other teachers we worked with, decided that we couldn't live with such circumstances any longer, that we needed to inquire into our classrooms in ways that described not only the celebrations, but also the concerns.

What complicates the telling of this story is that, in the classroom, it is never just one thing; it is many things. For instance, I would advise my student teachers that classroom management was not just the norms that got negotiated with the class, but included also room arrangement, tone of voice, classroom appearance, time of year, clothing choice, everyone's current emotional state, word choice, the current buzz in the cafeteria, the nature of the classwork, the nature of assessment, physical stance, and so forth. In other words, every decision made in and every stimulus that entered the classroom contributed in some way to the ongoing messages being sent about how the participants in this room managed the way they worked together. In addition, much of this activity occurred simultaneously and recursively. Therefore, it was hard to get a sense of what was causing what, what came first, and what happened in what sequential order.

In thinking about practice, my colleagues and I realized that we were part of many ongoing conversations. As noted in the next chapter, some of this dialogue was and remains interior, as we tried to make sense of practice through educational theory and research. However, other dialogues among ourselves occurred simultaneously with the interior dialogues, and often transacted with those discussions. The difficulty in recounting this process is that its linear progression is obscured by the simultaneous, transactional, and recursive nature of the discussions. There is no tidy formula that is followed. We go into a meaning-making mode that includes past, current, and future discussions. We don't perceive the problem, go to the literature, collect the data, analyze them, and implement new practice. It is more muddy than that and thankfully so, for I think the complexity forces caution and attention. Rarely is there one moment of epiphany where our purpose and direction come suddenly clear. Instead, our process is marked by a series of small "ahas"—some clustered on the same day and others separated by months; some part of a close-knit weave and others seemingly important but connected less distinctly.

In effect, I was and still am evolving my praxis, the transaction that occurs between theory and practice. Each shapes the other. My current understandings about how literacy is taught and learned shape decisions about my practice; my implementation of those decisions, aided by systematic reflection, further shapes my evolving theory. At times in this process, I have entered into a state of grace as theory and practice elegantly dialogued around me. At other times, I have limped along badly, aware of gaps and inconsistencies in the work of the classroom as it related to my theoretical understandings. Whatever the case, theory and practice continued to shape each other as my praxis evolved.

It is crucial that readers bear in mind that the overall complexity of the reflective process often takes on a linear appearance when described or when

they ascribe a linearity to it, perhaps because that aids their sense-making process. However, the reflective process in action would resemble, to my way of thinking, a loosely wound skein of coarse wool. To begin, the main cord itself is a coming together of associated elements combining individual qualities and structure into composite strength and form. The movement of this structure would be turned back on itself, intertwined, sometimes parallel, no doubt twisted, perhaps knotted, even snarled. And there would be these damned fine threads going off on their own all along the main cord, prickly to the touch, and unfinished in nature. A distant look would reveal a simple and whole structure, but any close inspection would yield the complexity. Finally, the main purpose of a skein is one of temporary organization. It is not an end in itself, but meant to hold these threads in that pattern until they can be woven into some other order. From my perspective, dialogue with colleagues about pedagogical issues of worth served to knit my various skeins of understanding into an intellectual comforter that knew no end.

REALITY, FICTION, AND TWO WEEKS IN THE HAMPTONS

As I segued from the 1980s into the 1990s, I found myself pondering my practice. Much like the skein of wool I described, my classroom appeared whole and functional on a distant look by a casual observer. Respect pervaded the room, students complied with and some even engaged in the work, and there was both quantitative and qualitative evidence of student achievement. But I had my concerns. The ethos of the school seemed to be one of apathy and distance. What counted as learning by too many of my students appeared too facile, rote, and compliant from my perspective. My intention to include issues of race and culture in my classroom and my attempts to understand the impact of such inclusion fell short of the depth of my expectations. The hope that education could provide economic and social advancement came to be questioned, at least on some level of cognizance, by both my students and myself. Finally, the mainstream culture paid attention to our school only when something went wrong, and then only to finger blame.

On the other hand, there was much about which to be hopeful, chiefly, the students themselves. They amazed me—sometimes merely by showing up, given the adversity some had to contend with in their daily lives. Others, when I could create an opportunity for such sharing, displayed a richness in their home life, a depth of family support, that destroyed the myth of shattered living situations often associated with low-income families. And daily, some student in some way would experience a breakthrough in learning that led me to believe that more was possible.

Still, the great spark in teaching that Mary Smith and my young junior high students had fanned within me was wavering, even though I literally taught right next door from the school where I had started my career. More and more, I found my locus of control lessened to the extent that I felt ineffective in my solitude. In many ways, I have always been an outsider—the Eastern European Catholic raised in German and Protestant neighborhoods, the working-class boy scheduled into college preparatory classes composed mainly of the children of professionals, the White teacher in a Black classroom. For this and other reasons, I had no history of being a joiner as I grew up and went through college. Instead, I became a keen reader of culture, needing to understand the codes or Discourse, what sociolinguist James Gee[3] equates to the language, social values, mores, and conventions of a culture, just enough so that I could create a space for myself without calling too much attention to myself in the process.

I carried this mode of understanding into my early teaching. Although I can remember wonderful discussions with many of my colleagues in those days at the start of my career, and I made much meaning from those talks, I remained, like many other teachers, the isolated practitioner. As I have heard many teachers say, when the chalk dust hits the fan, they close their classroom doors and work within the autonomy their well-managed classes and prompt paperwork have won them. So, too, did I.

But even with the door closed, the rising tide of apathy that had its origins outside my classroom seemed to seep into it with greater impact each year. As I noted, too often students gave themselves little credit for learning and held few expectations for that learning. Rather than redoubling my effort, I found myself doubting my capacity to find enough good in my practice to staunch that which threatened us all. Finding my classroom becoming an island in an encroaching sea of indifference, part of me grew tired of shoring the levy, part of me kept at the task, and a growing part of me wondered whether I needed a levy at all. Besides intrusions from beyond my classroom, what else was I holding at bay? In isolating myself from the outer disruptions, I also was denying myself outside support.

When I struggle, I usually turn to education. I sensed I needed to take a course. In the past, the intent of coursework was to pull me back to what mattered in my classroom. At this juncture, however, I felt a need to escape. Having always enjoyed writing, I thought maybe it was time to switch my teaching to automatic pilot, as I had seen some of my peers do, and seek some avocation that would fill in some other way the creative gaps I had long reserved for my teaching. In 1986, Long Island University offered an intensive summer institute: 2 weeks in July in the Hamptons studying fiction writing and listening to literary readings on a nightly basis. I opted in. It seemed exciting and I wasn't disappointed. With instructors, guest speakers, and the majority of students coming from the Manhattan literary scene, I was caught in the swirl of words and meaning that vibrated and crackled with enthusiasm. The air in the institute breathed promise and I came away not only feeling invigorated and validated as a writer, but suspecting that nothing anytime soon could top that experience.

SWIMMING WITH COLLEAGUES

When asked when I began to explore teaching through inquiry in more comprehensive ways, I can narrow the response to an exact date and year—August 1986, the month following the fiction writing institute. To an extent, I have always been moving toward greater inclusion of inquiry-based learning through my teaching. At Penn State, my undergraduate courses had been dominated by two somewhat contradictory threads—behavioral objectives and the guided discovery approach to teaching. Although I found little use for the former as a teacher, I was attracted to guided discovery and tried to implement it at times in my classroom. Although enactment of this approach assumed an answer toward which the teacher guided learners and thus seemed a sort of controlled inquiry, it did build upon theory that suggested that learners take greater ownership of understanding they come to on their own terms. Since my students always seemed more engaged when I used guided discovery, or approaches like gaming or values education that shared similar philosophical roots, I tried to incorporate such activities with greater frequency, although they often felt tangential to my overall practice.

As I learned to be a teacher during those first 5 years teaching language arts and reading in a junior high school, I was struck by how fragmented my instruction was. My methods professor at Penn State, Ernie Page, described English not as a subject, but as a predicament. I was living that description as I juggled atomistic skills-based instruction designed to help students improve their scores on the California Achievement Test (CAT), formulaic writing instruction to help students gain a greater sense of paragraphing, and more open-ended, inquiry-based instruction geared toward helping students to make meaning for themselves. Particularly troubling for me was that, despite showing improvement on the CAT and increased facility on the kinds of paragraphs we favored in the school, far too many students struggled to transfer their skills into other aspects of their lives and education. Too frequently their writing and reading in practice remained immature and static.

Knowing this, I sought help by attending Beaver College (now Acadia University) and getting a masters degree in composition. As I began this work in 1979, the idea of writing as a process was bursting on the educational scene.⁴ Prodded by educators such as Elaine Maimon and Richard Wertime, I explored ways to engage my students in writing through one-to-one conferences. This moving from the front of the room and working with students individually and personally changed the ethos of my classroom. Over time, students began to see writing as something that evolved through dialogue, engagement, and close examination. Each writing task became a problem to be solved, an inquiry, if you will, and—when it was working well—a dialogue among writer, teacher, and others. Yet, even though I implemented writing as inquiry in larger ways and began to make strong connections to reading as process, I still felt stifled by the structural and philosophical constraints of the school. I was inching toward making inquiry central to our work, but, cut off from others with like philosophy and experience and from structures that would support such work, the inquiry remained off-center and sporadic, particularly as my enthusiasm waned in the face of swelling apathy.

Curiously, despite my efforts in the Hamptons to de-emphasize my teaching in terms of my life efforts, I signed up for another institute that focused on the teaching of writing. Held in a cinderblock classroom in urban Philadelphia during the hottest month of the year, what was to become the first summer institute of PhilWP held little for me in the way of expectations. Having just come from an experience that had galvanized me in terms of my own potential, I started this August writing institute fully expecting to be underwhelmed and unfulfilled, especially since the School District of Philadelphia was a partial sponsor and I had long before come to mistrust their efforts.

Led by Susan Lytle of the University of Pennsylvania, the PhilWP summer institute closeted me for 10 full-day sessions with 31 other K–12 public school teachers, most of whom displayed the same range of hope and cynicism about urban teaching that I showed. Despite our concerns and perhaps due to able facilitation by Susan and her team, electricity soon crackled through that barebones classroom, and each day of our 2-week institute was one of discovery and affirmation. Among the many ideas the leadership team brought to the institute was a belief that we learn best when allowed to make meaning for ourselves. Through our mutual exploration of readings and our own teaching, we came to see the potential of taking an inquiry stance on our classrooms and what such a stance would mean.

As I let the waves of ideas that surfaced in that institute wash over me, I managed to catch hold of a starfish or two—one of them being the idea that I could no longer relegate inquiry to an off-and-on status. Instead, I had to pull inquiry to the center, to make it the way we worked as a class, and to see it as a means for taking that "predicament" and giving it a greater cohesion. Another was that there was much to be gained in the formal and informal discussions that occurred among colleagues, if one could focus on those dialogues through process and reflection. A month earlier, my literal romps in the waves off Long Island had helped to wash off the debris of the previous year. At the time, I thought the intent was to pilot me out of teaching. By the end of August, the PhilWP summer institute had me wading waist deep and then diving through the swells of pedagogy.

CREATING A SMALL LEARNING COMMUNITY

Although I can mark August 1986 as a great shift in my intentions, I can't say that my classroom changed radically, at least not at first. Other things had to occur or fall into place. But at least my inclination seemed firm. Two of the emerging support mechanisms for fostering a greater implementation of inquiry in my classroom were dependent on one another. One was my continued involvement in PhilWP and the second was my taking a sabbatical to work for the writing project while starting my doctoral studies in reading, writing, and literacy. Through both these efforts, I was invited to engage in dialogue with a range of significant theoretical and research readings, all of which pushed me to enlarge my conception of inquiry-based education and particularly to bring a political lens to such work. Dialogue with this literature helped me to understand the critical nature of my classroom, taking *critical* to mean both essential to and questioning of.

In addition to the importance of this literature dialogue—which I describe in the next chapter—of equal significance is that continued involvement with PhilWP and my doctoral studies allowed me to meet and engage with a diverse range of teaching professionals. In both local and national venues, I became associated with teachers and teacher advocates who were excited by the possibilities of urban education and who refused to be cowed by the bureaucracies and often racist policies that stood in our way. This involvement allowed me to network with teachers involved in the various sites and initiatives of the National Writing Project, the National Council of Teachers of English, and the Teacher Researcher Special Interest Group of the American Educational Research Association. Getting connected to such a diverse group of teachers, who not only cared passionately about their practices and the students they taught, but also inquired into the way they transacted with their practices and students, provided me with a menu of approaches for doing more of my own inquiring. It also engaged me in a multitude of contact zones where I crossed multiple borders of culture and deepened and broadened understanding with each crossing.

All of this interaction with teachers deeply committed to their profession provided support for me as reform initiatives began to surface for Philadelphia comprehensive high schools in the late 1980s. Buoyed by a $6 million grant from the Pew Memorial Trust and led with sensitivity and savvy by Michelle Fine and Jan Somerville, the Philadelphia Schools Collaborative sought to help faculty reimagine those schools that had been most adversely affected by the move toward academic, magnet, vocational, and alternative high schools. The comprehensive or neighborhood high school lay at the bottom of this hierarchy of school choices, and talented learners were encouraged by counselors and parents to avoid comprehensive high schools at all cost. The result was that too many students in the comprehensive high schools were there because they and their parents were unable to negotiate the various gatekeeping mechanisms that allowed entry into the other schools, hadn't received the necessary social and academic support to feel successful in school, or, having managed placement into an academic or magnet school, hadn't received the necessary social and academic support to comfortably remain there. Already many of these students had been sifted out of the tracks that led toward access to political, social, and economic power. Dropping them into a school like Simon Gratz, where they could easily get lost amid the throng of 2,000 students, seemed tantamount to sealing their fate long before they could be in a position to take control of their lives.

The Collaborative basically had two bottom lines for reform in the comprehensive high schools. These schools had to embrace shared decision making and they had to find ways to group students into smaller units. The expectation of shared decision making was that it would give parents, teachers, and students more say in the day-to-day and long-range structure, philosophy, and management of the school. Gathering students into smaller units—originally called charters, but renamed small learning communities—sought to personalize education so that parents, students, and teachers had greater access to and rapport among one another. Given access to a wide range of progressive and reform-minded ideas, SLCs could choose from these ideas as well as incorporate existing structures and come up with a school within a school that reflected the needs of its students and staff. Despite their commitment to education that resonated with rigor, inquiry, and multiculturalism, Michelle and Jan created a reform framework that allowed for SLCs that ranged from fairly traditional, center-of-the-box manifestations to those that nudged and crossed the boundaries of traditional conceptions of school. What mattered is that the SLC worked over time with a limited number of students and that the teaching in the SLC represented a negotiation among all stakeholders.

For Natalie Hiller, Marsha Pincus, and me, these reform initiatives provided an opportunity toward which we had been moving steadily for a number of years. Like Marsha and me, Natalie saw her classroom as a place for reflection. Having all been involved with PhilWP, we had come to recognize the importance of literacy and inquiry across the curriculum and had been searching for ways to deepen and broaden our implementation of these ideas. However, Natalie had come to teaching after years of working in business and brought the wealth of that experience to her science classes. Interested in helping students connect science to their worlds, Natalie created classes that were both hands-on and rich with problem-solving opportunities.

The reform efforts initiated by the Collaborative gave us outside-in philosophical and financial support to match our grass-roots efforts. Particularly for me, what really represented reform on the part of the Collaborative was that, at least for a while, the factory-model hierarchies that existed in schools and school districts were somewhat flattened. The voices of teachers, students, and parents counted and were being not only heard but validated as SLC after SLC created a space that grew out of the needs and theories of its stakeholders.

Over our Thanksgiving vacation and a subsequent long hotel dinner as snow fell outside, Natalie, Marsha, and I drafted a common philosophy that we wanted our SLC to realize. We would be heterogeneously grouped across supposed ability levels as well as grade levels. Therefore, as much as possible, each class would have students from all grades represented in the SLC and, no matter what their degree of school success had been to date, all students would be expected to engage in complicated ways with text and to understand the ways their learning situated them in reference to the world beyond the SLC. Students would be responsible for not only their own education, but that of others around them, and a range of collaborative learning situations would be enacted. Assessment in our SLC was to be as authentic as we could make it, and students would show their ability to learn and work independently by periodic performances. Undergirding all this was the intent to infuse African American and Caribbean American culture across the disciplines in order to give our students ways to see themselves in the content of formal education.

One omnipresent aspect of our SLC was that literacy and inquiry would be used in all classes to make meaning and we would implement the idea of an essential question, borrowed from the Coalition of Essential Schools,⁵ as a means for driving our curriculum. An essential question is one that, although appearing simple in form, actually is complicated in understanding. It should be a question that resonates across disciplines and facilitates exploration into a range of complicated issues from a variety of perspectives. It should be less answerable and more explorable. For example, one year our SLC asked what role patterns played in our lives, and another year we wondered what it meant to enact change. The key to these questions is that all teachers had to buy into the question and then, for at least some part of their curriculum, inquire into it.

We named the learning community Crossroads. One reason was that we saw our classrooms as places where learning intersected with the world beyond school and thus as crossroads for meaning making. Furthermore, we saw high school as a crossroad for many of our students, a place of decision making that would forever affect their lives. We wanted this crossroad to be truly a site of choice, where students selected paths that they were prepared to follow rather than accepting the road that offered the least resistance.

class not written itself — "where to go from here?" asked

From this philosophy of teaching and learning, the stakeholders of Crossroads changed the structures of their school. Sensing that we needed more contiguous and continuous time with students, the staff again accessed Coalition of Essential Schools archives and devised a schedule of double-period classes that shifted on what we called an A/B rotation. What this meant is that on an A day a student might have only English, history, and physical education, while on a B day she or he might have only math, science, and Spanish. Over the year the number of A and B days always balanced to within one day's difference. In addition, students frequently retained the same subject-area teachers for several years.

To graduate, students needed to complete a senior project that involved library, experimental, and qualitative research as well as an interpretive piece, a portfolio reflection, and a presentation to a panel of teachers, community members, and students. Driven by our essential question, teachers involved students in more and more collaborative learning situations and more frequently assessed students via a range of projects. New students coming to Crossroads frequently remarked with various degrees of appreciation or concern about how different Crossroads seemed from school as they knew it. One large difference, however, was how veteran students in the SLC informally and formally mentored new students, bringing them into what the learners likened to a family atmosphere, with the full range of meanings of family.

SLC family as family

Although the central philosophy of Crossroads was drafted largely by Natalie, Marsha, and me during those initial discussions, the actual implementation and refinement of those ideas were a group effort. Believing in the Collaborative's mantra of shared decision making, we evolved a system of leadership that represented a compromise between our desires and those of the school district and teachers' union. Within the SLC we struggled mightily, but eventually a form of self-government evolved that relied heavily on consensus. Our belief was that for any decision of import affecting the SLC, we needed to have consensus of the entire staff. Without all staff members buying in, our initiatives would be diluted by the lack of participation of those who voted in the minority. With our staff fluctuating between 15 and 18 people, gaining consensus was often difficult and it took years before we knew not only when to use consensus, but how best to navigate discussion once in

"looping" — teachers move w/students

a consensus-building process. Despite the struggles we had around leadership and having one's voice heard, Crossroads managed to remain an SLC whose decisions most often reflected the thoughts of all rather than most or some of the staff.

There were times all of us in Crossroads longed for faster, if less egalitarian, decision making. Each of us, at one time or another, felt silenced in our discussions. Yet, through the tensions created by multiple perspectives on our work, we built a sense of community that kept us all engaged in ongoing dialogue. The community we created was simultaneously unified and multivoiced. Any of us, teacher or student, could describe the basic tenets of Crossroads to a visitor and that depiction would be fairly constant. Yet we also knew each of us created our own vision of how those tenets played out and what they meant. For me, a teacher who valued his loner status, it was, to a great extent, this collegial give and take that allowed me to rethink my classroom. Because of that dialogue, I knew I would never be able to just close my door again.

4

Some of My Best Friends Are Theorists

It was a dreary music store. The walls looked as if they had been last painted at the end of World War II and then by using paint left over from naval destroyers. Fat-bodied electric guitars hung from the walls and the dingy showcases were crammed with mouthpieces, saxophone slings, picks, and violin bows strewn in no particular order and with no apparent effort to catch your eye. I usually would wait for my turn at instruction leafing through the yellowed sheet music, sending up swirls of dust to filter through the remaining light of a fading fall afternoon. But this day I just plopped down on an old amplifier, chewing my nails, knowing that I hadn't picked up the guitar once since my last weekly lesson.

Eventually, I trundled my three-quarter length Gibson down the dim hall at the back of the store to a tiny square of a room. My instructor managed a weak smile at the sight of me, dragged on his cigarette, and waited for me to fold myself into the folding chair behind the folding music stand. I flopped open my Mel-Bay guitar book and plucked at "Go Tell Aunt Rhody" and "All Through the Night," picking their melodies completely devoid of emotion as my instructor tried not to wince too visibly. Despite my dismal performance, he assigned another page in the instruction book, I packed up, and his next charge took my place on the folding chair.

It wasn't supposed to be this way. This was supposed to be the great love of my young life. As a child, tunes were always running through my head, if they weren't spinning on the 45 RPM portable player we kept in the dining room or the hi fi that took up residence in the living room. I knew show tunes, standards, drinking songs my father taught me, and the rock and roll that was just coming into its own. Plus, I had wanted that guitar ever since I found an old cowboy model my Uncle Andy had left in my grandmother's closet. It had taken me 6 years and false attempts on both the accordion and clarinet before I finally was given that battered old six-string just as I was turning 12 and starting junior high school.

But it seemed all for naught. On the ride home, my dad, tired of paying for lessons that seemed to be going nowhere yet again, delivered the news. That was the last dollar he was going to waste on guitar lessons. I didn't even make a pretense of protest. Mostly I just felt relieved that the ordeal was over and my time was my own again. When we got home, I packed my guitar into the closet and tried not to notice it when I dressed for school each day.

Sometime the following summer, I was given the fingering for four chords—C, F, Am, and G. Prior to this, all I had been shown were single notes for songs I had little interest in learning. However, when I was shown these four chords and told that, in the right sequence, I could strum out "Where Have All the Flowers Gone?" I plopped myself in my room and practiced those chords until I could both play and sing the song. I remember being fascinated by how easily these chords flowed together and how my strumming the rhythm so completely filled in the song. I would just ring out those chords repetitively , in different patterns, my ear planted on the curve of the body, reverberating with the strings.

Once, putting those chords through a sequence, I suddenly sat up. There was something familiar to the sound and the rhythm. I repeated the sequence and realized that I was approximating "If I Had a Hammer," a big Trini Lopez hit on the radio. Through further experimentation, I realized that these four chords could be combined into different patterns in different songs. If I listened to my records carefully, I could hear the chord changes under the lyrics and replicate them. Other chords were possible and certain patterns seemed to show up in certain types of songs. By making subtle shifts in my fingering, I could alter sound and reso-nance, making that which had been simple, more complex in nature. I sought out chord books to expand my patterns, and more experienced players to give me feedback on my playing. Suddenly, I was spending whole evenings in my room, banging away at those strings and playing as many folk, rock, and R & B songs as I could decipher.

MAKING MEANING

On a basic level, this opening vignette illustrates an old adage: Give hungry people a fish and they will eat for a day; teach them to fish and they will eat for the rest of their lives. My music teacher, as tolerant a man as he was, was feeding me fish, and fish I didn't even enjoy. However, when I discovered the patterns behind the music and could connect those patterns to music I wanted to play, suddenly I was fishing for myself in a stream of rhythm, harmony, and melody.

But more important, this story emphasizes for me the ways theory and practice dialogue both within and without the classroom. I'm not suggesting that the manner in which those initial chords were taught to me was any different from the way I had been taught single notes. Both were examples of direct instruction. It's what occurred next that became the inquiry and also, in retrospect, introduced me to the ways theory and practice transact. Since I was no longer fettered to a system of instruction, it was incumbent upon me to take my parcel of information, make sense of it, and then generalize about it. Given a motivation to continue, I could begin a dialogue between my musical theory and practice that would allow both to grow together. I could take those chords and, much like the strings beneath my fingers, bend them to my needs and find infinite ways to vary the outcomes. To this day, I still cannot read music to much result, but I can sit down with most popular guitar songs and work out chords and melodies within minutes of hearing them. Because I grasp the essential theory behind the way music is made on a guitar, I have learned how to exploit that theory in practice. And, as I drive my musical practice, I discover new theory about how music is constructed and played. The one cannot be considered without considering the other.

This vignette is a classic example of what motivation researcher Mihaly Csikszentmihalyi[1] has labeled the "flow" experience. He maintains that we learn best when we move beyond extrinsic reward and instead develop a sense of intrinsic motivation for whatever learning we seek. What enables this shift toward intrinsic motivation is our developing a sense of purpose for the activity and then using feedback gathered through both reflection on and outside observation of ourselves involved in the activity. As we dialogue with this feedback and develop more complicated theories about whatever it is we are doing, we eventually hit a level of sophistication in which we can blot out the world around us, such is our concentration and involvement. Csikszentmihalyi calls this "flow," as if the learner has entered a hard-rushing current and has been carried away. It's akin to what athletes frequently refer to as the "zone." Whatever the term, it suggests a state of engagement that is dependent on a transaction between theory and practice, one that benefits from some form of systematic and intentional observation and reflection.

This chapter focuses on the ways I dialogued with educational theory, particularly as I used those encounters to clarify my practice and then used my practice to clarify my theory. As such it views the interpretation and creation of theory as a necessary part of teaching and argues that teachers need to embrace these understandings on a conscious level in order to more overtly develop their teaching. My intent is to make an argument for the importance of theory in the practical everydayness of classrooms. Then I show how an ongoing dialogue with three theorists helped me to create a vision-in-process of a way of teaching that responded to and reconsidered the needs of my practice.

TRYING TO SIT ON A CLOUD

At various points in my teaching career, during some whole-faculty or departmental meeting, I might give my views on the topic under discussion. At these moments, I usually would try to connect my concerns with my current sense of my emerging teaching philosophy. Almost inevitably, another faculty member would weigh in with a comment that in some way tried to diminish what I had said by equating my thoughts to being able to sit on a cloud—it's a nice idea, but you can't really do it. Sometimes these comments were said with a gentle, yet paternal tone ("That's OK, son. Teach a little longer and you'll forget all those useless things you learned in teacher education) and at other times the tone was more one of utter impatience ("Is he done? Can we get back to practical matters?"). To be labeled a theorizer by some in my high school was akin to being called a liberal during Ronald Reagan's presidency.

This response, of seeing theory and philosophy as antithetical to practice, always befuddled me. From my perspective, there is nothing more practical than theory and philosophy. For me, they provide a basis on which I can make most key decisions. They also set goals toward which I am always aiming, if never reaching. Among theory, philosophy, and practice, I am forever in dialogue through my systematic and intentional inquiry.

I need to say here that, like most other teachers of my generation, I have a well-founded distrust of the academy. Many of our preservice courses did not prepare us for the highly charged and vastly changing classrooms of the late 1960s and early 1970s. Far too many studies denigrated the work of teachers and frequently blamed students for the mistakes of the system. Too much educational theory had no sense of what real classrooms, particularly urban classrooms in a changing United States, were like or were becoming. As I started my teaching career, too large a swatch of the mainstream academy, along with the administrative community, positioned itself as an all-knowing font of knowledge and, from the vantage of teachers, sought to infantalize and control them and their efforts.

In addition, having been raised in a working-class family, I often take a practical view of life. Work is done to meet needs. Security is preferred to risk. Holding something in your hand is better than holding it in your dreams. One reason I elected to be a teacher is that it provided a steady paycheck and a fair amount of job security. I decided to get my advanced degrees in education rather than in English because I have deep reservations about what I perceive as studying literature for study's sake. My sense of academic research is that unless teachers can find themselves in the work, then it isn't much use to education. Although I now filter my experience through a variety of perspectives, I still use this practical lens as one of my perspectives for making sense of what I encounter.

But neither of these cultural constructions—my distrust of the academy and my need to see concrete results of my efforts—prevents me from embracing theory and philosophy as integral to my life. If anything, they reinforce my need to use theory to refine philosophy because the former expects me to call ideas into question and the latter expects me to justify my efforts. As literacy theorist Frank Smith[2] and feminist activist bell hooks[3] theorize, we are all makers of theory, we all posit tentative understandings of the world, test them in various ways, and use those understandings to refine our philosophy-in-process. Both Smith and hooks, as well as I, are quick to point out that the theory and philosophy we speak of are not of the Grand Capital Letter variety. Instead, all who seek to make sense of their world are theory makers about how the world operates and further transact with theory to reconsider their philosophy-in-process.

This making of theory, from my perspective, seems to be universal, from the infant contemplating language to the dying person contemplating mortality. Even some of my high school colleagues who would say that they saw no use for theory were articulating a theory, although certainly an ironic one. Those involved in the book and PBS series, *A Parliament of Minds*[4] made clear that the degree to which individuals see themselves as philosophers is dependent merely on how consciously they embrace their thinking about philosophy. They argue that philosophy failed us in the Twentieth century by becoming a subject to be studied rather than a phenomenon to be experienced and considered. In the end, it's not a question of whether we theorize and philosophize—I know of no humans who don't—but to what extent we consciously involve ourselves in the process.

Therefore, my practice—all educational practice—maintains an ongoing dialogue with theory. The two transact with one another, continuing to shape one another as the process evolves. It is a process of looking not just without, but also within. As my theory and practice transact, creating what is known as praxis, I continue to develop my philosophy of teaching and learning, based on these ongoing transactions. My understanding of what occurs in classrooms is a result of my making meaning of my past and current experience.

AN ARGUMENT FOR THEORY

As I will discuss shortly, I view my classroom as a space where a range of theories are put into play, all of which get filtered through my experience. To me, this filtering is one reason why beliefs about teaching and learning spin out so differently across a range of classrooms. A teacher who endeavors to enact Nancy Atwell's[5] ideas of Writing Workshop is actually incapable of replicating those beliefs to the letter merely because the teacher is not Nancy Atwell and thus brings a different set of experiences and contexts to the implementation. In fact, it's my belief that the best that teacher—or any other teacher—could say is that her work is based on or is an adaptation of Atwell's work. The minute any teacher begins to muck with Writing Workshop, those ideas cease to belong solely to Nancy Atwell and instead become a manifestation of ongoing dialogue, continually in process and, as the literary theorist Mikhail Bakhtin[6] might suggest, "tasting" of all the other experiences of all the other teachers who have tried to enact Writing Workshop.

This "whistling down the lane" effect is why I believe reform often fails in school and why it's so important for teachers and schools to have a clearly expressed set of beliefs about teaching and learning. When a school administration mandates an approach like Writing Workshop, they're often setting themselves up for failure for reasons that have little to do with the approach in question or the quality of the faculty. Too often, as schools seek to adopt new approaches, they bring teachers into the process only once a decision for adoption has been made. In the rush to get the program up and running, teachers usually are given a session or two of professional development, a binder full of guidelines, and little else.

This way of working is problematic at each step of the way. First, keeping teachers out of the discussion until later in the process frequently results in lack of a match between the new approach and what is already occurring in schools. In addition, districts often *adopt* programs when they should *adapt*, meaning that they seek to merely replicate rather than matching the program to the skills, interests, resources, and beliefs of their teaching personnel. Finally, by ill-equipping teachers with knowledge about the new approach through inadequate professional development, districts create little opportunity for teachers to embrace the ideas. Training and passing knowledge are substituted for dialogue and understanding. Based on such practice, it's amazing that any substantive reform occurs.

Instead, if individual teachers are encouraged and given time to consider, dialogue with, and express theory, they will be better equipped to merge a new approach with their emerging theory or to see where such an approach is antithetical to all that has preceded it. By seeking to transact with theory, by acting as the prism through which theory gets defrayed, teachers engage in the idea of praxis. As such, theory informs practice and practice informs theory—it's not a one-way street—and classrooms become vital organisms, changing and growing through reflection and practice, rather than repositories for educational fads.

INVITING LOUISE

Up to this point, I've mentioned *transactions*, but have left that term minimally explained. I have borrowed and expanded this idea from the literary theory of Louise Rosenblatt.[7] In her view, text has no meaning in and of itself, but gains meaning only when a reader transacts with it. It is in transaction, in which readers shape new text based on their experiences, and the text shapes the readers' sense of themselves, that meaning, simultaneously social and personal, is made. She uses the term *transaction* rather than *interaction* because the former implies first a sense of mutual shaping and second a sense of context, a sense that more is in play than just a reader and a text. Instead, both have contexts of space and time that play out as reader and text shape one another. All readers bring their experience to bear upon texts that have their own social histories; in that moment of transaction, new texts and new readers are born.

My sense, however, is that Rosenblatt largely intended her transactional theory to apply to a concept of reading and writing that was primarily limited to printed texts. As my own views of terms such as *literacy*, *reading*, and *text* have been expanded, first by Paulo Freire[8] and more recently by the work of the New London Group,[9] I have begun to see the concept of transactions in a wider context. Basically, a transaction still occurs between a reader and a text; however, the definition of what counts as text has widened considerably. In my conception, anything from which we can make meaning counts as text. Therefore, printed media is text, but so is sculpture, a musical score, an urban bus station, and the cry of birds at twilight. Within a classroom, then, students may be reading "Letter from a Birmingham Jail" as they read the sounds of a basketball being bounced down the hall while they try to read the physical stance of the teacher as she answers a knock at the door.

To illustrate the concept of transaction, one can consider any card game, but for this example I will use pinochle. In my family, pinochle is more than a pastime; it's a metaphor for life. In the game, four players laying down one card each during the playing of a trick might be considered an interaction. However, seen as a transaction, something much more complex occurs. The first card determines the next card played and the juxtaposition of the first two cards determine the next choice. The following choice of cards owes much to the sequence that preceded it, with decisions based on scores, relationships, history of the game, and cards played, among other factors. The end of the game is changed because all these variables are in play and conditions keep changing. Cardholders might make predictable or surprising moves, the shuffle varies the circumstances, partners communicate in overt and tacit ways. All of this is there for the reading, and with each reading the circumstances vary and a new text is shaped. And all the players, based upon their individual readings, become new texts themselves.

By thinking of my classroom as a place where multiple transactions with multiple texts were occurring, I began to imagine a place where learning was always under construction and was based on our individual and collective experiences. Here's one example of what this consideration of transactional theory meant for me in practice. After reading a text written by any author, new students in my class frequently would look to me, hoping I would tell them the "hidden meaning," as they often described it. Instead, I would ask why they wanted to hear the perspective of "this skinny, middle-aged White guy" as the dominant and perhaps only interpretation of the text. Wouldn't their interpretations of the text be different from mine, since they were younger, African American, and possibly of a different gender—to cite just a few cultural differences? Therefore, if they read *Medea* or *Their Eyes Were Watching God*, what was significant and made meaning to them might differ from my thoughts about the text. Furthermore, in theory, if there were 30 of us in class, there might be 30 different perspectives on whatever text was in question. I would be glad to throw my perspective into the mix, but only once all other perspectives were out in dialogue, with all being entered into our charts and notes on the work. By withholding my transaction with the text, I was helping them call to the surface their own transactions and hopefully validating their perspectives at the same time.

Such a view of reading essentially posits that all experience is read one way or another and, in being read, meaning is made of that experience and subsequently used to interpret future reading. Learners experience and inquire into their world through a mesh of these reading transactions. By using this expanded view of reading, text, and transactions, I have been able to draw connections to a number of other theorists whose work informs my practice.

INVITING PAULO AND LISA

As noted, the ideas of many theorists were invited into my classroom. For the sake of example, however, I'm going to focus on the work of three theorists—the aforementioned Louise Rosenblatt along with Paulo Freire and Lisa Delpit—who I believe were key to my decision making as I rethought my practice and whose ideas help me to better explain what I think was occurring in my classroom.

Paulo Freire[10] was an educator who worked with the poor and oppressed in Brazil. His theories of critical pedagogy, much like Rosenblatt's ideas of transaction, were built on the significance of dialogue. Teachers are not expected to indoctrinate, train, sloganize, or otherwise fill up their students with unconsidered information. Instead, the transaction between teacher and student should be one in which the texts of the world are interrogated in a mutually empowering dialogue. In particular, teachers use the needs and experiences of marginalized students as a starting point for a dialogue that calls the oppressive status quo into question and helps learners and teachers to use their literacy as a means for negotiating social change. Freire's idea that we first read the world and then read the word, and that we continue to interpret both the word and the world throughout our lives, is very much akin to Rosenblatt's ideas of transaction. It also argues that the act of reading is intimately tied to our individual and social experience. Therefore, as learners dialogue and transact with a wide range of texts and come to make meaning for themselves, that newly constructed meaning enters into dialogue with the mainstream and other cultures.

As a teacher working with students who frequently were economically, socially, and politically estranged from the mainstream and whose culture was undervalued by those who most easily accessed that power, Freire's ideas gave me another reason to teach. If students and their families questioned the traditional economic arguments for school and literacy, then perhaps the purpose for engaging both lay in the creating of ways and means for accessing those mainstream power venues so long denied. Unlike Freire, who noted that the oppressed in Brazil were frequently unaware of the ways the system worked against them, I found many of my students fairly adept at critiquing the system. However, too frequently they also had nihilistic and fatalistic views about their ability to create either individual or societal change in the face of such organized oppression. Through the ideas of Freire, I and many other educators have been able to imagine classrooms where the purpose of our work was not to get the next story read and the next test completed, but instead was an ongoing inquiry into the relations among the students, the teacher, their culture, and the mainstream culture. The point was not to consume and give back facts; instead the intent was to nourish and support critical thought.

By seeing my classroom as a place where the students and I inquired into and dialogued around issues that called mainstream culture into question, I evolved a way of teaching that helped students use reading and writing as a means to further define themselves in relationship to the many worlds they encountered. For example, as we inquired into the issues and creative works of the Harlem Renaissance, students used readings and discussions of texts from that period to rethink, among many things, their understanding of that time, the role of African Americans during that period and in the current period, and their understandings of themselves in relationship to the issues under discussion in those texts. Students who read Claude McKay's "If We Must Die" or Dorothy West's "The Typewriter" did so not just to understand the text, but to come to some deeper understanding of themselves in relation to the issues raised by the text, and hopefully to develop a greater degree of agency in terms of dealing with those issues. Ultimately, all of the work in my classroom was geared to help students engage mainstream culture from their personal and critical perspective, rather than one of assimilation.

Thinking about and understanding these transactions between marginalized and mainstream cultures has been a significant part of the work of Lisa Delpit.[11] Arguing that not to teach the power codes to marginalized students is to doom them to a life in the margins, Delpit also maintained that ignoring that which students bring to the classroom—their heritage, cultures, family background, social identities, and the like—is to place additional impediments in the way of learning those mainstream codes. Furthermore, and a point often forgotten by conservative educators who cite her work, Delpit insisted that students whose culture and language differed markedly from that of the mainstream population needed to inquire into, dialogue with, and critique those mainstream codes. To put it another way, learners were to transact with language and culture, shaping and being shaped in the process.

Delpit's work created a large shift in the way I considered my classroom in terms of culture and language. In a manner that Freire would have applauded because it made the complacent mainstream justifiably uncomfortable, Delpit made reference to the need for marginalized students in this country to both access and critique power codes while celebrating home codes. It was her writings that ripped to the forefront of my consciousness that language learning is deeply embedded in culture, that we study culture as we study language, and that the literacy classroom can either discourage or invite students into these studies of language and identity. Furthermore, she argued that not to teach the mainstream codes—the talk and walk of those who traditionally have held political, economic, and social sway in the United States—is to continue to marginalize those who have already been relegated to the periphery. I needed to find ways, which she made sound so easy, to both celebrate the home code— the language and ways of understanding the world that students brought with them from home—and also help students have access to and a critical view of the power code, all in the same classroom.

By seeing my classroom as a place to celebrate home codes even as I helped students engage and critique power codes, I embarked on a journey into language, one that saw language as something to be investigated and the investigation as something from which choices could be made. This way of considering language is in stark contrast to traditional views of learning inviolate rules of grammar. Instead, I asked my students to be ethnographers of language, to collect samples of language from the world around them, and to study those samples in order to come to understandings about the way language worked, not just grammatically, but socially and politically as well. The resulting investigations helped students unearth the deep structure of language, to see the nuances of language choice, and to understand the many language codes they carried within them and what it meant to switch or not switch among those codes.

code switching

ROOM 256 AS SALON

A fellow PhilWP teacher, Shirley Brown, often expressed a desire for a return to the idea of a salon, a gathering of intellectuals around light refreshments to discuss things literary. If only in my imagination, my classroom was a literary salon of a type, for it was there I invited a range of the great minds in education to dialogue about my practice. Although the work of other theorists took part in these transactions that filtered through my experience, I set about in those early years of the Crossroads SLC primarily trying to figure out what my classroom would look like if Lisa Delpit, Louise Rosenblatt, and Paulo Freire had all been sitting around kibitzing. Even though all the dialoguing took place in my mind, my classroom was a crowded space because I felt that each of these theorists, while they had much to say to one another, was contending for primacy. What exactly did a Freirian/Delpitian/Rosenblattian classroom look like?

From my vantage, the theories discussed above build upon a transactional framework. The terminology may differ at times, but whether we talk about transactions or dialogue or investigations into culture, we who seek to make meaning are essentially positing that we shape and are shaped by our experiences. As such, learning is social and historical, building upon our own experience and that of others. Learning is also personal and we seek to understand ourselves in relationship to the world as we read the many and varied texts we encounter in the world. Reading is a primary means to make sense of our experience; we use it not only to decode and comprehend, but also to make meaning.

This unifying theory understands and implicates the cultural underpinnings of learning—both the ways dominant culture has been used by schools to exclude those less closely aligned with the mainstream and the ways understandings of the cultures students bring to school can and have been used to invite all cultures to dialogue and learn across borders. In the latter classrooms, the language of the dominant culture is shaped by the home codes of the students and teacher. Language becomes not a prescribed set of rules, but rather a topic for inquiry, discussion, and multiple perspectives.

Most critical for me, learning is an inquiry. As a teacher and learner, I call my world and my own stances into question, and expect my students to do the same. It is perhaps my one expectation. I tolerate a range of perspectives and will even give respect to those I see as racist or misogynistic, if the holder of a perspective is willing to bring that stance to interrogation. I make it clear how I disagree with such views and why, but try to provide a process and opportunity for inquiry that allows all of us to look more closely, more systematically, and through a range of lenses. If I believe in the power of inquiry and the primacy of culture, then I need to trust the process and let it work within my classroom.

Through all of this, the terms *teacher* and *learner* become problematic because the lines between traditional definitions of those words blur. If my classroom is one of inquiry, dialogue, and transaction, then I must inquire, dialogue, and transact as well. Nor can any of this be false inquiry, dialogue, and transaction; I must be shaped by the experience just as I expect my students to be shaped. I must call my own stances into question. I must risk my own writings and thoughts. I must use my authority as a way for us all to realize our own authoritorial stances rather than as a means to reify my educational fiefdom. The inquiry classroom is an active one that seeks authentic learning that reflects the needs and understanding of all participants.

The next four chapters attempt to put even more experiential flesh on the theoretical frameworks I've erected. In them, I show the ways in which I raised questions about my practice and the school community surrounding that practice and how I sought direction for my teaching through transactions with students, colleagues, and a range of other texts. Particularly, I connect these transactions to the ideas of Rosenblatt, Freire, and Delpit, the better to show how these theories transacted with my practice over time. In doing so, I map my encountering of academic dissonance and my response to that encounter. By documenting the issues raised by one teacher—in this case, me—and by explaining the rationales for inquiry I developed and the process I used to develop those rationales, perhaps I can help others make their own arguments for the necessity of taking an inquiry stance and seeing teaching as transaction. Most important, I show how these transactions helped me to evolve a way of teaching—what I call critical inquiry pedagogy.

5

Yo, Wazzup?

Lisa Delpit had ticked me off. There, far away in Alaska, or Harvard or wherever she was when I first read "Skills and Other Dilemmas of a Progressive Black Educator"[1] and "The Silenced Dialogue: Power and Pedagogy in Educating Other People's Children,"[2] she had made me angry. What was this about? She seemed to be attacking the way I had lived my life, diminishing it, sweeping it away. Who was she? What was her right?

I had worked hard to feel that I was accepted in the Black community in which I worked, that my students saw me as more than a tall, skinny White guy, that I was somehow different from so many of the other White guys who had taught them with what in the best description could be called indifference and in the worst could only be called racism.

Every September, it was the same battle. At one time in my career, students called it "taking your heart." No one had authority just because they were "teacher." Authority was granted only if you earned it, showed you knew how to be an authority or, more probably in the eyes of my students, authoritarian. You had to demonstrate that you had limits, couldn't be "gotten over on," weren't "frontin" or putting up a false façade, that most of all you were fair and consistent in your use of authority, and that you could be trusted and were sincere in your efforts.

I had learned all this through trial and error, through conferring with older colleagues, both Black and White, through listening to the chatter in the hallways and before class, by coming right out and asking students about student behavior when the behavior confused me.

I thought I was doing it, what Delpit said needed to occur, crossing those boundaries of race, learning from "other people's children" as I sought to understand "other people's children." So, if I was doing what

Delpit had suggested, then why did those articles make me so angry? Why did I read a few paragraphs, fume for awhile, and then read a few more? Why did I carry the articles around with me, literally and figuratively, as I ranted about her accusations. Surely, this couldn't be me. I was one of the good guys. As it turned out, Delpit's words "other people's children" are perhaps for me the three most important words to ever follow a colon.

It's here where I should write about the epiphany I had, where it all just clicked, where some bell went off in my head and I had that shattering glimpse of heaven. However, that's not the dramatic arc of this story. There was never "A time"; there was only "time."

Gradually, perhaps like fog lifting off the Georgia mornings I've come to appreciate, I began to see myself in Delpit's work. Partly this came about because what I have learned about myself is that when I seem to have unexplainable anger toward remarks that I can't see directed at me, then perhaps I'm denying the connection. When an article makes me get up and walk for reasons I can't put my finger on, then I can bet that the words have touched a tender spot I don't want to touch.

It took a while, but when I finally heard what Delpit was saying, I began to see me in what was being said and started to sketch a picture of the work that still needed to be done. So much of my crossing of these boundaries, of trying to understand the culture of the world in which I taught, had been about seeking my comfort. How could I fit in? Be accepted? Be seen as different from other White teachers I didn't want to emulate?

When I let myself listen to what Delpit was saying, I began to see what was missing. This was about transactions. It wasn't about me finding a comfort zone, although that was important. It wasn't about me knowing my students better in order to teach them better, although that too was important. Instead, it was about understanding that the many cultures in my classroom and in faculty meetings were constantly transacting with one another, and in those transactions learning occurs, and too much of it was occurring tacitly in my classroom. Whatever sense my students and I were making in those transactions, we were keeping to ourselves. If we were to really cross boundaries of culture, then we had to acknowledge what happened when we crossed those boundaries. We had to learn more about one another and, more important, share our perceptions. We had to be willing to interrogate each other, but we particularly had to be willing to interrogate ourselves, myself as much as anyone else. There could be attempts to make all of us feel comfortable, but at times we all had to share discomfort. Contact zones are like that.

MAKING MEANING

Delpit helped me to see the racist in me, the prejudice in all of us. It's what I didn't want to touch. It's what most of us—of all races—don't want to touch. It will always be a sore spot. It won't go away. But we have a choice of letting it cripple us and denying its crippling effect or inquiring into its pain in order to lessen its hold.

No European American with any kind of social conscience wants to admit to being a racist. It's a label that, rightly so, is seen with disdain. That's why you hear too many people begin statements in discussions that cross racial lines with, "I'm not a racist, but . . ." and then they go on to make some statement that betrays their racial ignorance. Too often that phrase is not an inquiry at all, but a veiled statement of perspective. It's not a question raised to invite dialogue, but a condemnation meant to seal off territory. If those who utter that phrase are honest with themselves and are truly seeking dialogue, perhaps what they should be saying is, "I am a product of a racist society, but am working to lessen its grip on me. Help me to understand by explaining this."

By not seeing ourselves as racist, we too easily fall into the trap of assuming we are somehow free of its hold. As Rosenblatt noted, total rejection without thought is its own conformity, and that once we label, or in this case, unlabel, we free ourselves of the responsibility of further inquiry. By not appending racist after our names, we, in essence, give ourselves permission to never look there again and thus limit our walk away from racism.

My family suffers from admitted and denied alcoholism. It affects all of us, even those of us who can drink one beer and walk away. One manner in which alcoholics and the families of alcoholics confront their alcoholism is to every day admit to being under the grip of alcoholism, to every day understand how they have to re-imagine an existence that isn't tinged by alcoholism. The paradox is that only by admitting to being an alcoholic can you control its grip on you.

The only way I could deal with my being a child of a racist society was to admit I was that child. Coming to terms with these issues helped make it possible for me to see that the inquiries I did with my students across racial and other boundaries were transactions that would contribute to mutual understandings of what it meant to live in a culturally diverse and culturally divided society. As the incident with the Giovanni poem illustrated, my bridge into these discussions of culture became language. By inquiring together into the ways language played out in our lives, both within and without the classroom, my students and I found a common language for starting to understand the range of ways our various cultures transacted inside and outside our complex lives. This chapter shows the range of these discussions through my transactions with four students.

A TEACHABLE, RESEARCHABLE MOMENT

Two years after that junior class had inquired into language as a result of experiencing the Giovanni poem, Kenya, a senior in our relatively new SLC, gave a vivid presentation that the students described in positive ways as being lively, natural, and engaging. The keyword for me is natural. The class felt her talk was particularly effective because she sounded relaxed and unstilted and spoke in a manner to which my students could relate. The effect was a "naturalness" to her speech that made her sound authentic or real; the syntax, grammar, and vocabulary choices matched the expectations of this audience for that speaker. In this community of students, being one's self rather than "frontin'" or putting up a façade was valued.

But there was also criticism of her talk. One student noted that Kenya had spoken in what he termed as Black English and that, when it came time for her to present for graded evaluation, she needed to switch to standard usage. I noted his comments on the chart we were keeping and continued seeking other responses. However, I became increasingly aware of a buzz occurring among a group of young women. When I asked the nature of their displeasure, Cria Henderson raised the question, "Why is Black English under the 'Needs Improvement' category?"

Almost simultaneously, a chorus of related questions sang out. Seizing the moment, Cria continued her pointed discussion. As I noted in my audio journal:

> Cria said, "If we saw how natural Kenya sounded and her audience is Black students, why shouldn't she be allowed to speak Black English? Now she sees [her usage] listed as needing improvement. The idea is that's something that she should change. And that's a problem."

Her point was that if we admired Kenya's naturalness of expression and how she seemed to be speaking in ways that allowed her to speak with confidence and ease, we would be misguided in asking her to speak standard English, particularly before this audience.

Seemingly prodded by this query, the class discussion spiraled out from there. We engaged a variety of issues, among them the nature of the relationship between language and the mainstream power structure, what acceptance of mainstream codes meant for speakers whose language and culture differed from those of the mainstream, the roles of English teachers and students of language, and what it meant to study the mainstream codes while celebrating the home codes. In our excitement, ideas were tumbling out one upon the other and we all were competing to hold the floor in order to make our collective points—so much so that when the bell rang, signaling the end of the school day, nearly half the class remained at their own choosing to continue the conversation.

As is often the case in classrooms, much of significance was happening simultaneously. To start, teaching and learning roles were being shifted. For at least this moment, the traditional teacher role as the seat of authority and information giver, and the traditional student role as passive receiver of knowledge, had been put aside. In like fashion, our individual racial identities—Black students and White teacher—gave way somewhat to a common group identity. We, as opposed to they and I, were trying to make sense of the issues at hand. Who we were, remained important, but what we were saying and how that contributed to a common understanding of these power issues became equally important. Yet we weren't undiscerning dreamers sleepwalking toward some soft pillow of consensus. Opinions were being challenged; new questions and circumstances were being raised.

But perhaps most significant for the purposes of this chapter, two realizations seemed to be dawning upon many of us there. The first was that what had been for too many students somewhat of an inquiry in name only, was now becoming an intentional inquiry in both purpose and deed. No longer merely an assignment to be completed solely because I had requested it, the inquiry was coming to be viewed as a personal need to be filled through academic means. As we transacted around issues generated by Kenya's predicament, many students were showing their first overt awareness of themselves as inquirers into language.

Second, we were all experiencing an understanding that language was open to inquiry and a multiplicity of perspectives. By wondering what Kenya's use of home codes in the classroom meant in terms of our language use and that of others, we were freeing ourselves of the prescriptive notion of language often fostered by traditional grammar texts and equally traditional classroom instruction. Instead, we were developing a sense that language use and impact could be described, that we could be the describers, that the use and impact were open to a variety of descriptions, and that the description rested somewhat within the control of the describer. We were evolving a sense that language was in process and that we were part of that process.

That this moment represents a pivotal teaching experience that we seized in our mutual investigation is enough to merit discussion. But for our purposes here, I believe that the events depicted above and the student inquiries I will profile below represent more than interesting snapshots into practice. Instead, I argue that the work represented here has much to say about language learning, about the ways students interact with the word and the world, and about the impact all this has on classrooms that aspire to supporting students who think and inquire critically. In particular, this chapter argues that as students gain an awareness of themselves as inquirers into language, they simultaneously make complex their perspectives on language and the ways language intersects with their lives. Furthermore, these transactions around language provided me and my students a means for crossing into contact zones of culture that, although not without risk, afforded us some level of safety as we tried to understand how race and language matter.

SETTING UP AN INQUIRY INTO LANGUAGE

At the time of the study, our essential question for the year was, How does learning connect you to your world? For the purposes of my literacy classroom, I adjusted that question to read as follows: How does learning about language connect you to your world? Using various fictional works (e.g., August Wilson's *Fences*, William Gibson's *The Miracle Worker*, Jamaica Kincaid's "Girl") as lenses, and assorted autobiographical works (e.g., Richard Wright's *Black Boy*, the film of Christy Brown's *My Left Foot*), as frames for our own compositions we raised questions about language and began to relate those questions to our lives. Eventually, this work led to a 3-month period when the students developed their own questions and, via interviews, observation, and audiotapings, developed personal inquiries into the impact of language in their lives and their community. In effect, we were moving from the personal to the academic and from theory into practice. And, of course, the whole process being recursive, we were reconnecting the academic to the personal and using our practice of language to raise new questions and develop new theory.

The preceding paragraph makes the process sound more orderly and deliberate than it was. As the work progressed over the year, I felt pushed by time to start that which was my intent all along—to have my students enact an inquiry into issues of language. However, rather than researching only through texts, I sought to have my students research through interviews, note taking, and audiotaping. Still, I resisted launching them into the research until the approaching spring signaled that time was becoming precious. Somewhat desperate to get moving, I held brainstorming sessions that generated lists of "what happens when" questions (e.g., What happens when the language of rap is studied for what it says about Black America? What happens when an African American speaks only standard English?) At last, we had begun the work, but next steps were unclear.

It was at this juncture that we had the discussion about Kenya and language choice. Spurred by the felt need rising in the room, I created a frame for taking their individual questions and enacting a course of inquiry. Using the brainstormed list as either a source or a guide, students were to find a question to call their own. Each would then conduct an initial interview with someone who could speak on issues related to her or his question. These interviews would be analyzed by groups in class and a plan for gathering more data would be strategized. This expanded data set also would be group-analyzed and a research report written. Finally, students would pull their inquiry together—the readings they had done earlier in the year and the qualitative research that had come at the end—into an essay that was based on their question and that argued for some action or stance to be taken concerning a language issue. Having that frame, we used the better part of 8 weeks fleshing it out, as I filled in the gaps by responding to the learning needs being generated by my students. *responding+growing+unexpected allow room for learning opportunities*

STUDENTS INQUIRING INTO LANGUAGE

In order to better understand the nature of a classroom that seeks critical uses of literacy, I offer profiles of three students who wondered how language intersected with their lives. Taken individually, these profiles detail the discrete ways these students evolved as learners, how they developed their own inquiries, and what they came to understand about language. Taken collectively, these profiles give us a larger image of the range of perspectives about language evident among these students and their peers, and the ways the same assignment evoked ranges of response, connection, and involvement.

Nora Jenks

As a learner, Nora Jenks was a cooperative, soft-spoken young woman who frequently seemed out of place in the rough and tumble atmosphere of our SLC. Her ideas of classroom behavior frequently differed from those of her more urbanized peers. For example, on a student response card commenting on life in the SLC, Nora wrote that what bothered her "is that some kids don't help each other as they need help. Why? Because if you say something, the kids laugh at you and that should not be." The concept of a classroom where students were more supportive of one another's efforts was not realized to the extent she would have preferred. As I would see frequently over the course of the 3 years I taught her, Nora was in a different place in relation to her peers and was frustrated by her solitary status. And although soft-spoken and polite, Nora was not a pushover. She held clear opinions about the ways life and learning should be conducted. However, she frequently kept those opinions to herself. But as the year progressed, she found response and reaction sheets to be an outlet for her frustrations and, in this manner, her beliefs became increasingly part of the class mix of ideas.

In addition, Nora represented a small, but continually growing, minority of students in the school who traced their roots to the various islands of the Caribbean. As speakers of dialect, these students coped with many of the same language challenges as their African American counterparts; however, their dialect also set them apart from their peers whose urban Black codes, while similar, can be markedly different from the codes of the islanders. Therefore, Nora brought perspectives to the classroom language issues that at times echoed what her peers said, but she also introduced new issues to be considered, as alluded to in this interview excerpt:

> I mean it's hard to change from a different way you speak when you're from another country. American way is hard. Most time when you try to speak you communicate with a person from a different country, they don't understand. They keep askin', "What did he say, what did he say?" Gets me annoyed.

As the quote indicates, learning "American"—whether customs, culture, and/or language—was not without trying circumstances, and the nature of those circumstances, and the ultimate effects on language learners were of interest to Nora because she had been down that road.

Despite attempts to fit in, Nora remained linguistically isolated, and this isolation was a theme that ran through both her oral and written work during the time of the study. In this regard, her research project at the end of the year was particularly telling in what it reveals about her sense of alienation. She was curious about how others adjusted to language change and what it meant for their lives. As she wrote:

> My question is: What happens when someone tries to adjust to a different form of language? I chose this question because I wanted to get an idea of how others have adjusted to a different form of language. I personally chose to do this because I wanted others to see the change I have been through.

This theme of coping with language change and difference continued through her work where she focused on how others have dealt with the problem. She noted:

> Mostly everyone said it was hard to adjust to a different English
> form of language. One person said, "I think it is hard because
> people speaks fast and I have to try to adjust as time past." Another
> person said, "It is kind of awkward at first, but I've learned to
> adjust myself." The third person said, "It's very hard because
> having spoken one form of language before, it is awkward trying to
> speak another one."

Eventually, Nora came to some understanding that dealing with language
difference was inevitable and compromise was perhaps necessary. As she
wrote in her reaction to her research project:

> I learned that having to adjust to a different English form of language
> takes time to adjust and if you want to fit in you have to be able to
> speak the way the people who are around you speak. By doing this
> project I learned that you should not have to change for good to
> please someone [but] it is good to switch at certain times when you
> are around certain people when you are speaking.

Whether Nora's remarks are read as expressing ambivalence or acceptance
about the need to shift among codes, what was evident was that she had
complicated her view of language. She now included responding to social
factors such as audience and purpose as part of her repertoire of consider-
ations prior to making an utterance.

This complexity, at least for the time being, left Nora in a linguistic limbo.
As the passages above indicate, her speech was a combination of a Caribbean
American dialect, Black urban codes, and standard English, none of which was
necessarily dominant. Not being linguistically comfortable with any one community, she seemed somewhat removed from all three. Her investigation had
made her aware that the ability to codeswitch could prove useful as she negotiated across communities. However, knowing this and doing this are not one
and the same. Like Kenya, Nora was conflicted between language choice that
is comfortable and identifiable to self and language choice that is preferred by
the mainstream, but uncomfortable in personal practice.

To seek some insight into this discomfort, Nora used our English class to
inquire into that conflict. By conducting inquiry into language difference and
the intolerance that accompanies such difference, she was able to vent her
own frustration and to become aware of some coping techniques. She also
was able to comprehend the complexities of the questions she was asking,
that these issues created a range of nuanced response that necessitated further investigation on her part. For example, in the following excerpt, Nora

was awash in possibility as the advice, even from people of her community, took on a complexity that forced her to examine her own situation:

> What stood out most in the interviews is that there is great support by each individual family on adjusting to a different form of language. The first person's interview said, "It is difficult for my family to accept my learning of a new language form, but my family supports me." Second person said, "My family told me that I shouldn't try to be like others, but be proud of who I am." Third person said, ". . . my family is a big help and encouragement to my change of language form."

The family support she uncovered took on a variety of shades. In one case, the family acknowledged the loss associated with switching between home and mainstream codes, but still advocated the need to do so. In another, the family voice was more ambiguous, urging that the learner be proud of who she was and reject conformity. However, it is unclear, through what Nora has given us, whether such advice meant the learner should retain the language of the home—be proud of who she or he was—or whether the advice was to shun paths of others and forge a unique and personal path of which to be proud. Whatever the implication, Nora was left to sift the responses for whatever continuity she could exact.

Rather than raising complex questions and arriving at simple answers, Nora instead had come to realize that the range of possibility concerning her situation was wide and that, instead of gaining clear consensus, she instead had a responsibility to make sense of the conflicts. In this instance, noting the common thread of family support running through her own research provided Nora with insight into ways to encourage her own language learning efforts, but the insight was directional rather than definitive. More inquiry would be needed.

Robert Turner

At the time of his participation in my classroom, Robert Turner was designated a special education student who was being mainstreamed with resource room support. He acknowledged that his chief problem was an inability to maintain attention, particularly in an oral environment, for any length of time. In effect, if left unaddressed, Robert would disengage, fade out, and glass over. Through the support of resource room personnel and his family, Robert had gained a modicum of control over his wanderings and was capable of functioning in a mainstream classroom if the teacher was sensitive to the need for keeping him engaged. As Robert put it in an autobiographical piece, if he remembered the voice of his resource room teacher repeating, "Focus, focus, focus," he could retain the concentration needed to complete schoolwork.

In relation to many of my other students, Robert Turner had experienced less academic success in school, had encountered fewer opportunities to consider language options, and had developed a history of language study that too often had consisted of remedial, skills-based work aimed at "fixing" his language deficiencies. His immersion in these borderlands of language had left him feeling somewhat isolated in terms of his relationship to the mainstream codes, and, on at least one occasion, he spoke of his emerging need for greater language flexibility.

> Black English is in my neighborhood because Black folks accept it. But there is a whole world out there besides the inner-city Black community and I should have a line of defense waiting for them.

These words, taken from a panel interview, reveal a speaker who was aware that language differences existed, but was only beginning to make sense of the ramifications presented by these differences. Seeking a "line of defense"—the words virtually leap from the page—Robert saw language as an attack from the outside that required some sort of battlement for his protection. By electing to leave himself open to language possibility, Robert sensed that he exposed a vulnerability and felt a need to protect himself against the dominating nature of mainstream codes. This sense of urgency brought on by an almost siege mentality and the degree to which he grappled with both the issues and usage of language, although perhaps more extreme in Robert, separated him only in degree, but not in perspective, from a great many of his peers.

In his report based on his own inquiry into these issues, Robert continued this investigation of language imposition from the outside by describing his own discomfort with standard English. He cited instances where he had made attempts to operate in the power codes and pointed out the paradox: If he would "try to speak as clear and correct as possible," it would result only in his "speaking unclear and in the process, stuttering." In essence, the harder he concentrated on *how* he was speaking, the more he was unable to render his thoughts with clarity or flux. This predicament connected Robert to Kenya, whose presentation and subsequent discussion he had observed. In effect, they are both caught in a linguistic Catch 22: They can opt for the home codes and appear natural—a sought-after attribute in this community of speakers—or they can opt for mainstream codes and be considered proper—a necessity for negotiating the mainstream culture; however, neither had much chance of being perceived as both natural and proper simultaneously, at least at this stage of their language development.

In trying to clarify his feelings about this conundrum, Robert likened it to a White who is conversant in mainstream codes, and nonconversant in any forms of Black dialect and/or slang, being placed into a language situation that involved having to cope with speaking and being corrected about the use of the latter language forms. The realities of current power relationships aside, Robert's point is that the White speaker described here, in trying to converse in Black codes, would appear less natural, more inarticulate, and less fluent. In addition, the speaker would show evidence of ambivalence about acquiring the codes. As Robert put it, ". . . [the White] would know—like I know—that there's no way he'd fit in."

On the other hand, Robert was quite aware that facility with one's home and/or neighborhood codes created opportunities for expression that were intimately and perhaps irrevocably tied to identity, both personal and cultural, as he indicated in the following written excerpt:

> If [Whites] knew Black English, then they would understand our music and how we use the sense of our ears to dance so well, and that it has nothing to do with our genes. They would understand rap music, that it is a pure mixture of Black English and slang, and the constant rumbling of beats which our sensitive ears follow. They would know that it is a constant use of emotional language, that when used well, pumps a lot of Black English speakers up and results in violence.

This passage is significant for a number of reasons. The first is that this text makes evident that Robert understood the interrelations of language and race and power. On some level, he connected the use of what he called "emotional language" to the use of violence. Although it's not clear if he was referring to the political provocation of someone like Malcolm X, the argument for leading the "thug life" popularized in hip hop, or the ability of one street tough to get a rise out of another, Robert believed that speakers of Black codes possessed a capacity to move others to action. There was a fundamental belief in the capacity of language to affect people and of African American speakers to use that capacity to their advantage.

In addition, like Nora earlier, Robert was uncovering the complexity of these issues. As he discussed the ways language was connected to various aspects of African American culture, he was uncovering a deep structure for himself that associated knowing with multiple perspectives, which he continued to investigate even as he attempted to shift those burgeoning theories into practice in his daily life. To this end, Robert appeared to be a student of language, and through his investigation, he expressed concern for what was lost as he codeswitched. But it didn't stop there. His connections grew even more complex. He acknowledged the rhythm of language as an influence on Black art and music. He connected Black English to Black slang and what he called "the constant rumbling of beats which our sensitive ears follow." With deep emotion that transcends the flat transcript, he urged Whites to understand and accept Black codes in order to better understand and accept Black culture.

As Robert engaged more and more with the process of inquiry, he was simultaneously making his understanding of these concepts more complex and asking others to consider his arguments and beliefs. Those same arguments and beliefs he was sharing, were undergoing refinement and re-examination through contact with the ideas of others. By examining White speakers coping with Black English, Robert created room for discussion of his many diverse language threads. As his comments indicate, he was sorting out the intricacies of what it meant to codeswitch from a form of Black dialect to standard English, even as he struggled to function in and accept those codes.

To that end, there is evidence here that Robert, like many other students, was trying on different ideas, as it were, testing them in public, and then assessing their viability. At the same time he was becoming surer of his class voice and, in a similar fashion, was experimenting with opening up in class in order to gather peer critique. As he wrote on a reaction card, Robert enjoyed our inquiry transactions because, "We learn individually, then we speak out and comment orally, learning how to communicate and share, and to be proud of our work all at the same time." There was a deliberate intent on his part to use the processes of the class to further both his inquiry into language and his ability to function in an academic situation.

Cria Henderson

Another example of the ways students identified and investigated personal inquiries is offered by Cria Henderson, a young woman who had attended parochial schools through the end of tenth grade, but was finishing out her secondary education in our SLC. Although many of her family members were professionals, she was very much part of the working-class neighborhood of the school and was popular among her peers. In this manner, she was one of an ever-growing set of my students who were proud of how well they functioned in the classroom and yet maintained popular status in the adolescent community. She brought a certain vibrancy to the classroom and a willingness to engage in discussions that, because they crossed various boundaries such as those of race and gender, could be construed as risky. Yet she did so in a manner that was open and forthcoming.

She was also a caring learner, one who was quick to spot and scrutinize an injustice. As documented earlier, it was Cria and her friends who interceded on Kenya's behalf. Among the first to make connections between our classroom inquiry and her own life, Cria sought ways to continue to personalize our work. In this manner, our inquiry into language struck a chord within her and she saw this as an opportunity to examine her own language background in order to consider what this meant for her language future.

As a result of the class discussion of Black English, Cria decided to investigate what happens when a Black American speaks only standard English. By interviewing and observing African American users of standard English, Cria came to the following understanding:

> Out of the project, I noticed that it's important to learn standard English. There's nothing really wrong with it. It can help out. But it's also important to know Black English and speak the language in your community. And I have to agree with [Robert] that most Blacks think Black slang is Black English and that's confusing. Black English is more than running around sayin', "Yo, wazzup?" all day. So I think it is important to learn more about Black English.

She, like Nora and Robert, was now using data that she had collected to help form her conclusion.

This use of data to inform her opinions became quite evident in our discussions subsequent to her inquiry. She peppered her argument with examples culled from her research. For example, despite the pragmatism of her acceptance of standard English as a force to be reckoned with, Cria rejected its dominance and the way its users devalued and excluded variation. Although she could see the value of a universally accepted code of English, she doubted whether the current standard acted as such. As the next interview excerpt indicates, Cria could draw upon her personal experience and make two arguments: The first allowed room for a common version of English, but the second suggested that the current standard was more exclusive than inclusive.

> The school I went to before I came here was [a Catholic school] and I went there from the ninth to tenth grade. And there was more White people than there is Black. And you know, bein' around White people I found myself pickin' up, you know, how they spoke. They have their own words that are quirks. But when I came here, for the eleventh and twelfth grade, and I started this project, I noticed that standard is the base language. This supposed ta be the language where everybody is supposed ta understand. You can speak how you speak, around where you wanna speak. But say you're comin' to where somebody doesn't speak the way you speak, and you wanna get your point across, that's when you supposed to bring in the standard English. That's why I think standard English was all

brought about. But see, the thing is, White people created standard English. They didn't say, "Oh let's have a Black person represented for the Black people. Let's have a Chinese person represented . . ."

The last two sentences above give a clear indication of Cria's question: If there is going to be a standard, couldn't that standard be more evocative of the rich diversity present in the country?

Cria's main position was that it was important for Black speakers to retain a firm grip on the home codes among which they were raised. Taking on fluency in mainstream codes was acceptable for maneuvering in that community, but retaining home codes for communication, particularly in the Black working-class community, was equally important. As was made clear by many of my students, one should never forget the language and the ways of one's first nurturers. To illustrate this, Cria spoke about a family member—her aunt—who had, from Cria's point of view, strayed too far across a racial and, perhaps, class boundary and now saw standard English not as an option, but as a preference.

> My aunt on my dad's side, she speaks standard English all the time. And when I go over there, she corrects me all the time. "It's not *you ain't*, it's *you're not*. If I had a dime for every time you said *you ain't*, I could be the richest woman on this earth." And she even makes fun of how we speak (unclear) and laughs about it. I don't think it's really funny, for real for real. I think she's lost her whole background. It seems like when I see her, I don't see a Black aunt, I see a White aunt. That's what I see. A creation of learning back in her day. I think she was one of maybe four or five Blacks that graduated from [a catholic school]. But learning that Black English is wrong and how you talk is wrong and this English is right, and you're learning from mostly White teachers, you come up to be like her, speaking standard English, speaking like White people or their language.

Of particular note here is how Cria examined the causes of what she construed as the aunt's defection and centered her concerns on the aunt's educational situation, as Cria put it, "a creation of learning back in her day." The use of this phrase gives us a sense of the way Cria viewed the impact of education, that somewhere in her theory of how we learn, we are a product of our environment, of our peer and adult influences, and of the values taught or indoctrinated into us. According to Cria, the aunt was virtually powerless against the forces around her because the aunt had few options. By growing up in the 1950s and 1960s and encountering mostly White teachers and White peers, she would have had little choice but to accept mainstream codes without critique.

Cria, however, seemed braced not to allow the same to happen to her. Her comments indicate that she was unhappy with her aunt's attitudes and was particularly concerned that her aunt used language difference as a point of contention and as a means for belittlement. Furthermore, Cria attached this belittlement to language use she most often associated with the dominant culture, another strike against it. It may not be true that, as Cria indicated, the aunt has "lost her whole background," and it is prudent to consider that what constitutes Blackness or Whiteness, although certainly connected to language, is in no way limited to language. But what we have here is a clear example of what language educator Geneva Smitherman[3] has identified as the way language issues divide the majority of members of the Black working class from the majority of Black professionals, with Black academics vacillating in the middle. The Ebonics debate sparked by the decisions of the Oakland School District was this division writ large. But in this microcosm caused by Cria's investigation into language, she expressed a theory that students learn language from adults and peers in their sphere of influence, but that students, if informed of the possibilities, have some agency in terms of language acquisition and that acquisition should include a retained fluency in the home language as well as an acquired fluency in the power code.

Whether or not we agree with Cria's theories, we need to accept that Cria, like so many other of my students, was a theorizer, a role she supported through analysis of her experience. This theorizing took place regardless of what went on in the classroom; however, the classroom investigation gave her opportunity, tools, and a forum to systematize, intentionalize, and thereby deepen her role of theorizer. In Cria's personal inquiry, there was evidence of the young woman calling upon earlier discussion and work in the class, using that work to form a question for inquiry, and then using that inquiry to inform her stance on the issues. All this was sparked by the discussion of Kenya's presentation, but the background for these issues came as a result of our year-long foregrounding of language. In essence, Cria, like so many other of her classmates, made her theories of language complex by holding discussions with texts, with teachers, and with students, and through her systematically gathered and reflected upon experience.

SEEING LANGUAGE DIFFERENTLY

When, a few years earlier, my students and I had investigated language as one result of reading the Giovanni poem, we had embarked on an investigation that was both spontaneous and prefigured. By the time my students reacted to the poem, I had been reading and discussing Delpit's work and part of me was ready to rethink the ways we explored language in my classroom. Still, I was in no way sure how or when to enact that work. Like me falling into Mary Smith's classroom all those many years ago, the Giovanni poem reading, too, fell into fertile ground. My students and I were prime for exploration and just needed the right conditions to get us started.

The investigation in which Nora, Robert, and Cria participated, in comparison, was more preplanned. I entered the year intent on studying language throughout both semesters. Still, like all good inquiries, this one responded to the needs and concerns of students and was not without its own spontaneous pivotal moments, as this chapter illustrates. Although somewhat dissimilar, these inquiries share two key ingredients: Both were in response to issues raised by Delpit and both allowed students to see the role of language in their lives differently.

[Ultimately, these students began to see language in complex and involved ways.] The more we investigated the use of language in Black and White communities, the more able we became to see language not simply in black and white terms, pun fully intended. Despite some reticence, Nora came to realize that her Caribbean dialect and power code could co-exist within her, as could other codes she encountered in life. It was no longer a case of either/or, but was in the process of becoming more contingent on for whom, when, and with what purpose. In a similar vein, Robert grasped that many codes were within his reach, but also grasped that these codes brought advantages and costs. He came to realize that it was difficult at best to operate and sound natural in a language code with which one had little practice using or had mixed feelings about acquiring. Cria, perhaps more than the other two, came into our discussions with a fairly complicated view of language based on her experiences; however, she made these views even more complex. Language became a means for making sense of the world around her and deepening her views of race and its impact in society. She began to see ways in which language defined us as individuals and as groups, and the way such definition could open possibilities and close doors.

As I have noted, Delpit raised important questions for me about my classrooms. [One of the questions involved how best to help my students simultaneously learn *and* critique the power codes. What I learned was that, for these students and others like them, it was not a matter of *if* they were able to speak and write in the mainstream codes—they could and did at various times in my classroom—but was more a matter of figuring out why they would feel disposed to do so. A key factor was motivation. The students were deepening their awareness of the role language played in their lives. In doing so, they were confronting whatever reluctance and reservation they might have had for more consistent use of the mainstream codes of power.] Nora, Robert, and Cria each expressed concerns that learning to negotiate mainstream codes didn't always support and celebrate the ways they talked at home or among peers. This dissonance presented them with moral and practical dilemmas.

In addition, although they were each coming to some acceptance of the need to speak and write in different ways to different audiences, putting that thought into action was difficult. This difficulty was evident for a number of reasons, but chiefly they felt that, as they shifted their language in different situations, they also shifted their conceptions of who they were—and that shifting was problematic. This contributed to at least an unwillingness on their part to gain greater fluency in the power codes. To paraphrase Freire, before *accepting* the word, students must *accept* the world that goes with that word, an act that is not always easy, culturally supported, or sought.

Also, by engaging in these inquiries, the students deepened their understanding not only of language, but also of themselves as serious learners. Nora was able to find a means through which she could come to terms with language concerns and also air her views to the class, thus getting beyond the role of silent observer. Robert, who self-admittedly had trouble focusing on schoolwork for long periods of time, was able to harness his attention and pursue his inquiry into Black English in ways that both affirmed and problematized his thinking. Cria, already fairly comfortable with academic critique and discussion, nonetheless came to realize how a systematic and intentional inquiry into her own experience could enhance the collected experience of the class, and that her opinion backed by documented experience seemed to count for more in the world. By giving themselves the room to enlarge their self-vision, these students were able to act in ways that validated that vision. By opening themselves to consider the ways the power of language had been used against them, they opened themselves to generating ways that same power could be put to their use.

For me, part and parcel of this discussion was a realization that the sustaining of multiple perspectives, and not a push for consensus, was perhaps the sought-after state of an inquiry classroom. It was in these discussions, fueled somewhat by critiques of Freire's work that worried that a critical classroom needed to support a range of viewpoints rather than a single critique,[4] that I began to open my room more to a range of opinion. Diversity of opinion was to be not only tolerated, but encouraged, as long as that opinion was born of extensive attempts to gather a diversity of evidence on which to base it. It was I who introduced the term *Black English* into the classroom, along with the work and positive intentions of African American educators[5] who saw Black English as a language to be celebrated. It was I who felt sure that the majority of my students, most of whom were fluent in a range of Black vernacular, would seize upon these beliefs and make them their own. Such was not the case, as a range of views on this subject emerged from my students.

Still, I found myself arguing for these views, almost insisting that my students weren't thinking logically, until I began to understand that the argument wasn't mine to make or not make, although it was within my rights to raise. Nor was it the job of my students to either roll over and placidly accept it or dig in their heels. Instead, the purpose of our inquiry was to engage in substantive dialogue that, through close examination of the word and the world, elicited a range of opinion, perhaps as many opinions as there were participants in the class. What was important was not that we all took the same thing away from the class, but that we all struggled to find something worth taking.

Finally, this study reminded me of how difficult, yet how absolutely necessary, it is to venture across cultural and personal boundaries in classrooms. It also helped to clarify for me that race was only one of many cultural boundaries being crossed on any given day. Through the course of the year, we discussed the politics of the racist slur *nigger*, the effects of verbal abuse, language used by teachers and students when confronting one another, the language of self-identification (e.g., colored people, people of color, Whites, Caucasians, etc.), the power of profanity, and other topics of language controversy. Each topic had its hidden minefield that could have exploded or imploded our discussions. Yet, each also had rich pockets of unrefined ore waiting to be discovered and mined. Day to day and class to class, I held my breath worrying what might be unearthed and how we might handle it. Most times, I worried in vain. Purposefully bringing a topic, no matter how initially worrisome it might seem, into the fluorescent glow of our inquiry classroom always seemed more worthwhile than allowing it to tacitly control our discussion, hidden away just below the surface of our intent.

CODA

Those of us who teach in classrooms where the potential for crossing boundaries of culture are great—and we all teach in such classrooms—need to take inquiry stances in order to better understand what occurs when we do. As Delpit and others argue, we should find ways for students to celebrate their home language while acquiring and critiquing the power codes, something uniquely suited for inquiry. However, my experience with Kenya, Nora, Robert, and Cria suggests that because students maintain a range of ambivalence about both this celebration and acquisition, teachers need to encourage students to problematize and seek personal understanding of this ambivalence. I agree with educators who argue that not to teach the power code is to risk further marginalization for already marginalized students. To do otherwise would be wrongheaded on my part. However, I also argue that to dismiss resistance to power code acquisition on the part of speakers whose home codes differ from that of the mainstream as mere reluctance or, worse yet, inability to learn, is to diminish the depth to which this resistance runs. Furthermore, such dismissal sets up a cycle of circumstances that will continue to create further resentment and thus further avoidance of fluency in the power code.

Long after I had convened productive dialogue with most of the issues raised by Delpit's work, one nagging inference stayed with me. Should teachers of one culture teach students of another culture? That struck me to the core of my existence. Had what I had been doing all those years been wrong? Should I really have been teaching in a White school (we know they exist even if by law they should have gone the way of the opaque projector)? I called my work into question. In particular, I worried about what it meant to be a White male teacher of Black males. I could believe in my students and support their inquiries into the texts of their world, but my ability to be a role model was limited by the frame of my experience. I'm not a Black male and I'm not a guy's guy, whatever that is. But both experiences were desired by the majority of my male students. So was I the right teacher for them?

By the time I was lucky enough to spend time with Lisa Delpit at the Urban Sites Writing Network of the National Writing Project, I no longer needed the answer she provided for us. I had come to it through my own inquiry. It didn't matter that I was a White teacher of Black students. What mattered was what I did as a White teacher of Black students.

6

Why Are You Doing This?

Early in the fall of 1997 in what was to be my last year as a high school English teacher, a colleague approached me about matters concerning our SLC. As she turned to leave, she noticed a list hanging on the bulletin board. The words—Lubavitcher, Shabbas, torah, rabbi, and rebbe, among others—all had connections to Judaism. Being Jewish and knowing I wasn't, she asked me how I was using the list. I explained that my students and I were investigating tensions that had existed between Lubavitchers—a small orthodox sect of Judaism—and the working-class Black community in the Crown Heights section of Brooklyn, New York. The polite smile on her face turned down at the corners and she heaved a sigh. "Why are you doing this?" she asked. "Are you looking for extremism?" I noted that, on the contrary, my students, who themselves were Caribbean American and African American, were to act as a task force entering the community to gain a more complex understanding of the problems and strengths and to offer suggestions for easing tensions. The intent was to help us deepen our knowledge of culture and conflict rather than going on knee-jerk reactions and surface stereotypes. The teacher sighed again and shrugged. "You're just going to stir up a lot of anti-Semitic talk," she said as she walked out.

MAKING MEANING

The inquiry I tried to enact with these students seemed to have posed a threat for this teacher. Rather than opening dialogue around issues of race and social justice, she saw us instead opening a can of worms or Pandora's box, loosing upon the SLC things better left unsaid. Furthermore, our exchange had resurrected in me feelings of dread that I had managed to calm prior to this.

I had suspected this study might cause concern within the SLC; this incident only confirmed that. As I watched my colleague disappear from the room, I was left figuring out what to do next. On the one hand, I couldn't ignore her concerns. Yet, I also couldn't ignore the substantive learning potential that a close inquiry into these issues would bring.

As she noted, this work *did* possess the threat of creating an anti-Semitic *zeitgeist*; however, the same work also held potential for deepening our understanding of the complexities of racism and ethnism. But the possibilities didn't stop there. This work also could make some students feel so threatened by world realities that they would withdraw still further into the comfort of their already established mind-sets; alternatively, it could engage those students in the possibilities of transactions across cultures and encourage them to venture into unfamiliar, but enlivening, thought. More locally, this work threatened to undo several years' worth of community building within my class. Then again, this work possessed the potential to extend that community in ways we hadn't imagined. To an extent, I was feeling threatened by my own practice and how my decisions on my practice could create threatening situations for others. On the other hand, the potential of the inquiry excited me and I knew it possessed the power to engage us all.

Ultimately, in some way, to some degree, and with at least one or another participant in the inquiry, the full range of threat and potential for engagement described above was realized. Within and without the classroom, I saw a range of response that evidenced various degrees of threat and engagement. Accordingly, this chapter, by examining my work, that of a student teacher, and that of the urban secondary students we taught, illustrates the ways in which threat transacts with inquiry and critique. Centered on vignettes that emerged from our collective investigation into the concerns and circumstances surrounding Crown Heights, I focus on ways in which those involved saw inquiry as a process within which threat transacted. Therefore, threat—in this case, literacy events in which one's sense of reality, belief, and/or identity feels imperiled—is not necessarily seen as a disabler of learning. Instead, it is viewed as one of many possible elements in a classroom where students and teachers inquire. As I argue, threat is an element to be acknowledged and transcended rather than denied, ignored, minimized, or euphemized.

I'm not suggesting threat as a teaching strategy. Instead, I argue that educators recognize the dynamics of threat and how they operate in schools, how they are exacerbated by teaching through inquiry, and yet how such teaching allows for working through and beyond threat. Specifically, this chapter focuses on the ways adults and students in the program felt both threatened and impelled by the inquiry work we were doing. In inquiring into issues of race, ethnicity, class, and religion, stakeholders in the SLC felt that their world views, their value systems, and/or their levels of ideological and psychic comfort and security sometimes were threatened by those issues. This chapter is one attempt to understand the ramifications of those discussions. It also illustrates the ways in which the ideas of Freire, Delpit, and Rosenblatt continued to dialogue within my practice.

ACKNOWLEDGING THREAT

As I began to share my work about issues of threat in inquiry classrooms, I encountered resistance to these arguments from strangers and trusted colleagues alike. In some ways, it was similar to when I first shared my investigations into my students' perceptions of language and language learning. At that time, the resistance came mostly from African American teachers and, in looking back, I see it was rightly so. At the time, my first reaction to this resistance was confusion, because once again I thought I was getting mixed messages. By this time, having embraced what I construed to be Delpit's message, I was doing all I could to learn about the culture of my students through my students. My option to conduct teacher research was a manifestation of this intent, and my sharing of my tentative understandings with diverse audiences was further evidence of my seeking multiple perspectives on what I saw occurring in my classroom. Yet, African Americans, with fair regularity and both politely and not, were suggesting that perhaps I was poking my nose where I had no business looking. *Diff. Ways of Knowing* ← *Emic v. Etic*

However, when I fell back on my PhilWP experiences and stopped defending my position—listening instead to the concerns being raised—I began to understand the nature of those concerns and how I might be able to address them. The main issue being raised by African American colleagues was that they couldn't see me in the research, couldn't understand what connection I had to these issues other than to be one more White male mucking about in Black culture for what appeared to them the mere sake of study. What seemed so obvious to me—the fact that I taught these students I was studying— seemed obscured by the questionable history of White study of Black populations. Completely unaddressed by me was that my interest into these issues stemmed from my own working-class roots and my own issues surrounding the ways the power code had been used against me and others like me. By showing how my personal history had been affected by language and emphasizing how my study of language in the classroom was about transactions between students *and* me, I found that the degree of threat posed by my study was lessened for most African Americans viewing my work.

So when educators, both Black and White, raised questions about my discussion of threat in inquiry classrooms, I was still somewhat surprised, but not unprepared for coping with their concerns. Again, by listening to their issues, I began to understand that this notion of threat—the power of the word itself, in some cases—felt somehow, well, threatening. There has been an acceptance among many progressive educators about the need to create "nonthreatening classrooms." For example, Sorenson,[1] in describing her attempts to teach in democratic ways, noted that "establishing an open, nonthreatening classroom environment allows teachers and students to share the ownership of knowing," and that "teaching students to be empowered starts with a nonthreatening classroom environment." Somewhat like the stigma of racist, no well-meaning teacher likes seeing him- or herself tagged as threatening. Even my colleague Marsha Pincus, someone who so often has agreed with my line of thought in the past, suggested that she had problems with this notion of threat and that perhaps it was a male thing. However, she emailed me a few days later documenting an incident in her classroom where some male students had felt threatened by her classroom presence.

What I took from these concerns is that if I were to posit that threat exists to some degree in all classrooms, and especially those where students inquire and critique, then I had to frame that argument in ways that would allow readers to get past the negative impact of the word. As I noted above, I'm not trying to say that teachers should cultivate threat, but instead should recognize that it exists in classrooms where students routinely are required to use literacy to inquire into their world, and, rather than denying its existence, should use inquiry to help class participants transcend threat. One way to do this is to examine the theoretical base for inquiry that acknowledges the existence of threat in working classrooms.

In particular, Freire is quite open about the ways in which class participants can feel threatened when they inquire. On this point, Freire and Macedo[2] urge educators never to mistake the dialogue needed for sustaining what they call critical pedagogy as one that creates "a vacuous, feel-good comfort zone." Instead, learners—and by that I mean both students and teachers—in a Freirian classroom understand how difficult making meaning can be and realize that "studying is a demanding occupation, in the process of which we will encounter pain, pleasure, victory, defeat, doubt, and happiness."[3] Under such conditions, students and teachers can encounter threat that is posed by the raising of and inquiring into issues surrounding oppression. Freire and Macedo remind educators that such inquiries particularly cause those students in the mainstream culture to feel threatened as their privilege comes under scrutiny. And, to an extent, Freire argues that *conscientizacao*, or the learning to perceive social and political contradictions, can threaten the sense of self-denial that some who are oppressed might see as a secure, if passive, state. Rather than trying to minimize such feelings of threat, Freire and Macedo[4] urge educators to stay the course because inquiry will help those who hail from mainstream authority structures to realize that "certain groups such as African Americans are born and live always without any comfort zone, much less the privilege to assume they can negotiate the appropriate comfort zone."

I argue that educators who ask their students to critique as they inquire need to complicate their understanding of the dynamics of threat as these dynamics operate through their teaching, so that more of our students can embrace and thus transcend that which threatens. This is key because my experience as a teacher educator informs me that fear of creating a sense of threat frequently prevents well-intentioned teachers and students from developing their capacity as inquirers who critique. Furthermore, even this discussion of the theory that informed my classroom indicates that degrees of threat are inherent in the enactment of such teaching. Therefore, we need to address threat rather than deny its imposition.

A CLASSROOM INQUIRY: CROWN HEIGHTS, 1991

Within Crossroads, our inquiry-based emphasis was most evident in the use of an essential question to drive our curriculum. Consequently, the work in my English class was begun as a response to the question, What is change? With racial tensions transacting in the Grays Ferry neighborhood of Philadelphia, it seemed useful to conduct a critical inquiry into similar incidents that occurred in the Crown Heights section of Brooklyn, New York City in and around 1991. This Crown Heights inquiry was one segment in a series of inquiries into the nature of community change. Prior to this inquiry, we conducted an investigation into the dynamics of change in school communities. Investigations subsequent to our Crown Heights work included explorations into cultural changes inherent in *Romeo and Juliet* and the attempts at social change pushed by the activists of the Harlem Renaissance. In effect, the students were using each investigation to answer the larger essential question and were gathering data through the year in this effort.

For those who may not know, the racial and ethnic situation in Crown Heights was a volatile one in the summer of 1991. Tensions had grown to extreme proportions between Lubavitcher Jews, a small and uniquely orthodox sect of Judaism, and Blacks, chiefly Caribbean Americans, who shared the neighborhood. Key to the disturbances that happened in August that year was an incident in which the third car in a Lubavitcher entourage ran a red light, was hit by cross traffic, and crashed onto the sidewalk, injuring a young Black girl and killing her younger cousin. The Black community, already enraged by what they perceived as preferential treatment bestowed by the city upon the Lubavitchers, saw this accident as a criminal act that they feared

wmt on change! (margin annotation)

would not be prosecuted. Various acts of violence ensued, the most extreme of which involved an Australian Jewish scholar who had been nowhere near the traffic accident, but was stabbed to death by a roving group of young Blacks.

Each of my four classes, 112 students in all, was expected to complicate their understanding of these events. Heterogeneously grouped across sup-posed ability and grade levels, students divided themselves into small groups that also crossed grade levels, ability levels, and gender. Each group was instructed to see itself as a task force coming into this community to try to help ease the tensions in evidence there.

To seed interest and get things rolling, I used an audiotape of Anna Deavere Smith's *Fires in the Mirror*, which chronicles the Crown Heights incidents. The use of an audiotape was deliberate because I wanted the students to focus on the spoken language and not the visuals. In essence, Deavere Smith con-ducted interviews and, using verbatim excerpts, recreated these people onstage in a series of linked monologues. I used five monologues to show the range of opinion inherent in the Lubavitcher community and five to represent the same in the African/Caribbean American community. Students charted these monologues in terms of what was learned about the speaker, what came to be known about these events, what we learned about the community, what the speaker believed, and what the speaker called into question. We then shared information from individual charts to make a composite chart and, as the charts began to layer, started looking across them. This became our baseline data.

At this point, each group proceeded on its own, devising a plan for fur-ther data gathering, distributing responsibility among group members, and in-creasing their knowledge base. Students accessed websites, found a variety of periodical articles on the subject, worked through books on Caribbean American culture as well as Lubavitcher Jewish culture, discovered pieces on the history of Black and Jewish relations in the United States, and con-tacted or attempted contact with sources within these communities both in Philadelphia and New York. All this information was compiled into a writ-ten report that was submitted for evaluation and a group presentation be-fore a simulated audience of community stakeholders. Begun in mid-October, the work was completed by winter break, with only a self-evaluation to be completed in the new year.

A MOTHER'S CONCERNS

About midway into our investigation into racial tensions in Crown Heights, a mother approached me on Parents' Night. A thought-ful woman with a soft-spoken quality, she identified herself as

Mrs. Templeton, the mother of Teisha, an equally thoughtful and soft-spoken young woman in my class. Electing to stand, she stood over me and inquired into the progress of her daughter. I remember regretting my decision to remain seated, but answered her queries as thoroughly as I could. She seemed poised to go, but hesitated and finally asked about the nature of the inquiry we were conducting, and I explained much as I did above. She shook her head slightly and frowned. "I don't know if Teisha will like that," she said softly, but firmly. "It sounds harsher than what we speak of at home. I think she will be uncomfortable." Then Mrs. Templeton added, as if she had been talking with the colleague I described in the opening vignette of the chapter, "Why are you doing this?"

As a Euro-American male in a school populated by African Americans and Caribbean Americans, I had learned to look for ways to balance my beliefs about pedagogy and content with the ways those beliefs might seem threatening to the culture of my students. As Delpit and others suggest, I have asked my students and African American colleagues for perspectives on issues in my practice that might give me other ways of understanding how my work might be perceived. One glitch that occurs with this line of inquiry is that, as was noted in our language investigation, some issues divide the Black community in ways that make coming to a consensus very difficult.

Being confronted by this well-meaning mother, I sensed both her feeling threatened and the threat of her words. Not that Mrs. Templeton was in any way overtly threatening, but the issue she raised is one that I know frequently causes teachers to flinch from study that seems too politically obvious. They ask, What if parents object? What if someone gets offended? Here was a parent and she was objecting. Furthermore, the next day she called my principal to get his views on the matter. Threat, polite and respectable, but threat nonetheless was operating on two levels. Mrs. Templeton felt our study was threatening the sheltered atmosphere she had created for her daughter, and I felt that Mrs. Templeton was threatening my right to make decisions about pedagogy and content in my class. And I had to wonder whether I had a right even to ask her daughter to consider the questions we were raising.

Consequently, I went to Teisha and offered her an alternative investigation, one that I would negotiate with her and her mother, but one that would mean she would have to do much of this work on her own. Mrs. Templeton allowed Teisha to stay involved with the Crown Heights work. But the incident served as a reminder that issues such as these can threaten parents and students, and we need to inquire into their concerns, even if the raising of those concerns might threaten our sense of control over our classrooms.

The incident also caused and still causes me to wonder why none of my African American colleagues weighed in on the subject of my work. As the chapter opening vignette indicates, at least one Jewish colleague raised concerns. However, this colleague and I were somewhat professionally distant—genial in our relations, but little else. On the other hand, I had developed close professional and personal ties with other Jewish teachers. Although they ultimately supported my work in this area by providing me with resources and acting as sounding boards for my concerns, they also cautioned me that this work would "bring out misconceptions about Jews and Jews in America and Black and Jewish relationships." In particular, there was worry that students would generalize views that might be manifestations of only the conservative Lubavitcher community across the diverse strata of Judaism. These same colleagues also worried that students would offer uninterrogated opinions and that relativism would reign. Therefore, some stereotypical depiction might be written off as harmless opinion. Despite these worries, these Jewish colleagues believed deeply enough in the process of inquiry to support my efforts, having forewarned me about these concerns.

Yet, no African American colleague had expressed concerns to me. As indicated earlier, they had come forth with opinions when I investigated issues of dialect, as they had when I first had students explore the Harlem Renaissance. One explanation is that perhaps they had no concerns and another is that they may have decided to trust the process despite their concerns. A third explanation is that they had felt that I hadn't heeded their past concerns and so elected to remain quiet.

A fourth explanation is that perhaps my role as one of two SLC coordinators in the program created a situation where my African American colleagues felt they couldn't raise concerns. As a European American male whose religious affiliation could best be described as indifferent, I coordinated our SLC with a European American female who was devoutly Roman Catholic. The remaining 15 faculty members were either Jewish (eight staff members) or African American (seven staff members), and the SLC's student population was, as noted, 100% African American and Caribbean American. Therefore, the SLC represented a contact zone with all the potential for possibility and risk.

To an extent, it could be argued that as coordinator I represented the dominant and thus oppressive mainstream culture. But it is more complicated than that. First, in the school, the dominant culture was African American, with the leadership of the school entirely middle-class African Americans. So I may have been a representative of mainstream dominance outside the school, but that culture could be a liability within the school. In addition, although I could and do sometimes benefit from the privilege accorded White males in this country, I am really not a full-fledged member of that fraternity. My family is from Eastern Europe and has a very different value set and cultural history than those of Western Europeans. In addition, I'm a third-generation immigrant who grew up in working-class neighborhoods. Although other marginalized people might mistake me for a member of the power elite, few members of that elite have trouble seeing me as anything more than a pretender to the throne. In addition, I had helped to establish and enact a policy of shared decision making within the SLC. Therefore, my role as coordinator and cofounder of the SLC, although it was accorded some deference, usually did not deter anyone on the SLC staff from voicing their concerns to me.

I can only speculate as to why my Jewish colleagues chose to discuss their sense of threat with me and my African American colleagues either experienced no sense of threat or opted not to share it with me. The bottom line is that some of the faculty and at least one parent felt that by looking into racial tensions between Jews and Black, I was disrupting a tacit peace that existed within the school, one that suggested we stakeholders ignore the controversy rather than confront it. As Freire and Macedo suggest, some who raised concerns may have feared losing the comfort zone, even though such comfort often was purchased at the cost of critique and engagement.

Despite leaving myself open to charges of cultural voyeurism and even of being a provocateur, I elected to proceed with the inquiry. I was not surprised by the concerns; previous experiences had prepared me for the possibilities. Working closely with a range of teachers in various local and national venues had given me insight into how such inquiry could give teachers pause for any number of credible reasons. Therefore, I had to give these concerns heed and to gauge if the level of threat was more than I could expect these stakeholders to accept. However, my same leadership work also had provided me with the experience to suggest that sincere efforts at dialogue across perspectives could evoke at least an attitude of tolerance from those with concerns. Sensing this was the case, I decided to continue the inquiry because, as the inquiry evolved, I believed the value of such work outweighed the risks, as the next vignette suggests.

TRUTH AS WE PERCEIVE IT

One part of our process involved the charting of ten characterizations from Fires in the Mirror. *After listening to seven of these characterizations, we began a discussion concerning what we were coming to know. As we listened to these stories told from a range of perspectives, the triggering incidents of the death by auto and subsequent stabbing attack were described over and over by witnesses and community leaders. Each telling had points that all the other tales contained, but each telling also revealed points that others either chose to ignore or left off inadvertently. As we heard the words of each informant, we heard the story told as they knew it or chose to tell it. It became clear that one well-told tale frequently contradicted someone else's equally fervent version. Much like transparency overlays, each telling complicated the issues, and as we came to have more accumulated data, we also seemed to have less understanding.*

During the discussion of the seventh characterization, as often happened when students were struggling to make their concerns clear, I sensed an undercurrent among the students. Particularly, one corner of the room seemed abuzz with animated discussion. This continued until one young woman, Tai, with a pained expression and a world-weary voice, asked, "But what is the truth?"

On the surface, this might seem to be an exciting occurrence. And I have characterized it as the closest I had ever come to catching lightning in a bottle. The discussion that ignited from this query snapped like electricity through the class. Students became fascinated by the idea of having multiple truths and what that might mean for their own construction and sense of truth. As my journal recorded:

> And that became the germ of our discussion in that class for quite a while. What is the truth and how do we know what is the truth? The concept of truth is relative. Some people would say that truth is in the eye of the beholder. . . . Do we need the truth? . . . So many questions raised around that idea.

Suddenly this was not just an inquiry into racial and ethnic tension, although that was significant enough. Now this was also an inquiry into the meaning of truth, how truth is perceived, what truth is believed, and how beliefs indicate directions to be followed. Without having read poststructural theory, these students had begun construction of a poststructural stance on their world.

Yet, I argue that this moment of academic excitement was triggered by a sense of threat that had been evolving throughout our investigation. Tai's construction of truth as being fixed and attainable was being threatened, shaken from its moorings by the many contradictory truths spinning out before the class. Tai didn't state which version she construed as true. Instead, she asked for a clarification of what might be the truth because each telling held details that at least smacked of some sense of truth to her. Furthermore, she also was coming to a realization that no one in that room, not even me—her teacher—could really answer her question for her. In that plaintive request and my decision to let the class discuss the issue, Tai and others were coming to understand that they somehow would have to figure out the truth for themselves and that task felt daunting and most probably threatening.

Again, having one's beliefs threatened can cause a range of reactions, one of them being the taking of a defensive posture that permits no other views to be heard, much less considered. Tai and most of the rest of the class opted instead to immerse themselves in the ongoing discussion and to open their views to self-interrogation. The invitation to dialogue in a Freirian tradition provided a means for transcending whatever threat they felt connected to their own belief system and encouraged them to continue to investigate despite the shaky intellectual landscape.

I frequently sensed that in moments like these, students were expressing a vulnerability too often unseen in classrooms. They were saying, "I'm not sure about this. Help me." It is what Lindfors[5] would describe as an inquiry event. At these times, the part of me that dislikes seeing anyone struggle wants to come out with a definitive answer and put his or her struggle to rest. But I understand by doing that I'm only postponing that struggle and probably projecting a description of learning to which I don't ascribe. So partly because of my belief that we need to support students through their learning struggles, no matter how much the struggle might threaten their existing belief system, I turned the question to the class. However, I also made that decision because I really didn't know what the truth was nor do I think I could have stood in the way of an inquiry that had been building among the students for some time. In the complicated set of transactions that are inquiry classrooms, I both exercised my authority to call the topic and deferred to the authority the students had assumed for themselves.

THINGS NOT TAUGHT IN METHODS COURSES

Students in groups were examining an excerpt from A Taste of Power, *an autobiography of Elaine Brown who grew up in North Philadelphia and became a driving force in the Black Panthers. The students were expected to chart and discuss details of the author's complicated relationship with Jewish friends. Rachel Ravreby, my student teacher that year, picks up the story in her dialogue journal.*

As I began to turn my attention to [one] group, I heard Todd say, with disdain, "You know all these teachers is Jews anyway." I was waiting, eavesdropping really, to see what else they would say when Marisol raised her hand.

"Ms. Ravreby," she said, "is you a Jew?"

"Ah, why do you ask?" I replied suspiciously.

"I mean, are you a Jew or are you pure White? We know that Mr. Fecho is a Jew; are you one too?"

For the first time in 3 weeks I felt uncomfortable. I felt as though I was standing in this weird intersection where my personal, political, and professional selves were on display. I stumbled for a second, contemplating how I wanted to respond, wondering what would be the appropriate response. (I can't imagine any of the teacher training books covering this issue: "How best to respond when a student asks you a question that not only probes your personal life, but confronts our notions of race, religion, and ethnicity.") Eventually, I replied, in a tone of strained calm, "My father is Jewish and my mother is Christian, but I am not religious," and quickly moved to another group.

That she had a visceral response to this incident is clearly indicated by Rachel's word choice: *disdain, suspiciously, probes, strained.* My belief is that this incident threatened Rachel in several ways. First, her authority as a teacher was threatened by a question that seemed to blur the line between what was and what wasn't appropriate to ask a teacher. This raised a crisis of conflict within her that pitted her wanting to be forthcoming against a need to protect information she felt was hers to keep private. Also this incident threatened Rachel's evolving positive sense of this particular small group. As she noted, she had been in the school for only 3 weeks and was trying to construct an image of her classes that was built upon the strengths of her students. The views offered by these students upset her and caused her to at least wonder about the intent of the discussion. Were these innocent, offhand observations, or was malice intended?

Additionally, her concept of herself as teacher was threatened because her ultimate response was far more cursory than she might have wanted it to be. This became a moment of decision, one of hundreds that occur daily in classrooms where inquiry is fostered. Among her many choices, Rachel could have opted to reserve her right to privacy, could have chosen to problematize these assumptions and enter into the dialogue with the group, could have answered the question and moved on, or—as she did— could have answered the question and moved away in order to reflect on a course of future action.

Further complicating matters is the understanding that my relationship to Rachel, no matter how collegial we worked to make it, remained one of teacher to student teacher, especially so early in the school year. The line of inquiry was my choice, and my expectation was that she would participate. Again, if she had reservations about participating in this inquiry, she kept them to herself. We did negotiate a team teaching situation that gradually would grant her more responsibility for the class, but for the most part my decision to deal with such sensitive issues connected to literacy and identity had placed her into a situation early in her student teaching stint where her sense of self in the classroom was, at least to some degree, threatened.

I want to be clear that this discussion is not trying to determine whether or not Rachel made the "right" decision, whatever that would be. Instead, this is an examination of the decision she made in relation to the degree of threat she was feeling. Also, it is important to note that this was not an inquiry lost; it was an inquiry postponed. Once an inquiry stance is enacted in the classroom, multiple inquiries—both formal and informal—occur simultaneously. In addition to investigating racial and ethnic tensions that led to an inquiry into the nature of what we hold to be true, the group of students who asked Rachel these questions was inquiring into the backgrounds of their teachers, perhaps trying to detect other agendas for the original investigation. It is not farfetched to conjecture that at least some students felt some degree of threat and suspicion regarding what was largely my decision to investigate what Shipler[6] has described as the mercurial relationships between Blacks and Jews in America. This vignette is some evidence of that possibility.

A fourth inquiry that resulted was Rachel's need to understand her practice, using this incident as one of the lenses for looking. Rather than seeing these students as being unwilling to interrogate their own beliefs or using her stirred emotions to harbor ill will against them, Rachel elected to problematize the incident as a means of understanding and complicating her relationship toward her students. By writing about it in the dialogue journal she shared with me and making it the subject of subsequent discussions, including this writing, Rachel pulled both of us into an inquiry that helped her to transcend her sense of threat caused by the discussion.

In effect, Rachel and I decided to trust the inquiry process. We needed to use time and the work to best effect. On one level, this meant the two of us continuing to problematize class events that raised questions for us. On another level, it meant working with students in ways that acknowledged their comments—uninterrogated as some might seem—but also encouraged the subsequent self- and group interrogation of these comments. The intention was to establish a pattern or way of working that routinized deepening and detailing of expressed thought. Therefore, more ideas, whether they met with general agreement or not, were prodded for depth of interrogation. All learners, teachers and students, were expected to find corroborating evidence or ideas from other sources that backed their assertions.

NARROWING VIEWPOINTS

After taking part in nearly 3 months of intensive inquiry into sensitive subject areas, I asked students to respond to several questions that had them evaluate their work and reactions to our Crown Heights investiga-

tion. One of the questions asked students to consider what they had
learned from all this close looking. Two young women, Betty and
Lavonya, had been fairly active and involved in the work throughout the
study. They also had seemed to express working views of racial and
ethnic prejudice that struck me as both forthcoming and open to other
perspectives. Yet they both wrote responses to the reaction question that
filled me with doubt about our project. They wrote:

> *As a young black in Philadelphia, I would think differently about the*
> *Jews because of the ways they acted towards blacks and others. I*
> *would think that they are racist and that they only wanted to be to*
> *themselves. (Betty)*

> *Crown Heights . . . made me feel kind of upset because of all the lack*
> *of communication which was leading to riots, killings, and also a lot*
> *of stereotyping. . . . Crown Heights also made me feel that if you go*
> *there no Jews will like you because of your race. Even though you*
> *have done nothing. (Lavonya)*

To an extent, my own worries and those expressed by some of my colleagues are made evident in Betty's and Lavonya's concerns. Rather than
being opened to the possibility of dialogue with other cultures, these two
young women felt threatened by what they perceived as a lack of dialogue.
This was the result, even though we had spent nearly 3 months enacting these
investigations, had inquired into a diverse range of perspectives and attitudes,
had shown the ways in which some in both the Lubavitcher and Black communities were dialoguing in fruitful ways across cultural boundaries, and had
encouraged ourselves to brainstorm our own cross-cultural dialogues. Out
of over 80 responses on the self-evaluations, these were the only two students who had expressed what I would call a retro-reaction—one that seemed
to make them less open to possibilities inherent in contact zones. Yet their
response can't be diminished. Even only two occurrences of this retro-reaction
must be taken seriously because they so counter the intent of the inquiry.
Furthermore, others may have felt the same way but been too threatened to
respond in this manner by whatever asymmetrical relations of power they
perceived between them and me.

Taken within the context of this neighborhood and these students, this
response by Betty and Lavonya, although disquieting, was not completely
unexpected. Before we started our investigation into the tensions that pervaded Crown Heights, I did an informal survey of my students, asking
whether they felt racism could be limited. I purposely had chosen the word

limited instead of the word *ended* because past experience had informed me that most of my students believed racism was a fact of life, as certain as the routine police harassment they encountered in their neighborhoods. Still, even using the word *limited*, an overwhelming majority, prior to our inquiry, said that racism could not be curtailed. Little changed even after 3 months of discussing these issues. On a second asking of this question, over half of the students still felt racism was beyond reduction.

Within our Crown Heights study, one way an individual might feel threatened by the ideas being investigated was when the issues discussed seemed too large and thus beyond one's locus of control. The reaction of Betty and Lavonya is a good example of this. The investigation heightened their feelings of difference in negative ways and left them perhaps feeling powerless. The roots of racism seemed so deep that their sense of agency to act upon these forces was negated.

In some way, perhaps I hadn't established my support role concretely enough with Betty and Lavonya. Feeling too much on their own, they may have elected to regroup and reify rather than dialogue and transact. If they saw me as a facilitator in this inquiry, it didn't seem to be a vivid enough image to invite them to posit their concerns. Despite any number of ongoing opportunities to express what troubled them, they elected to share this at a time when it was too late for me to act. Even as I write about it here, I wonder whether more could have been done had I had an earlier inkling of what they were experiencing. I also wonder whether it had taken all that time for these young women to feel comfortable enough in our relationship for them even to bring this sense of threat to my attention.

DEEPENING PERSPECTIVES

Julie was in her third year in our SLC, coming with her older sister to our urban school after spending time in schools in Puerto Rico and other places where her parents had been stationed in their naval careers. Having lived in more culturally mixed communities than most of our students had, Julie had a perspective on issues raised by the Crown Heights and other inquiries that seemed more informed by those other communities than it did by her current urban neighborhood. Still, she was an accepted and respected member of our urban SLC who had both embraced and been embraced by the vibrant Black urban culture surrounding her. She therefore was positioned somewhat within and without this community. Perhaps because of this positioning, as she responded to the self-evaluation question about what she had learned through our investigation of these issues, she raised questions about herself and the students around her.

The Crown Heights situations have made me aware of fellow classmate's feelings on certain issues and concerns. I have noticed that not all of my classmates are as open-minded as I thought and many don't believe in half of the things that I do. As a student you learn many things pertaining to many problems, but I have now begun to notice that everyday I am surrounded by people who instigate and cause these problems.

[The Crown Heights work] showed me how cruel and stupid people get when tragedies occur. This project showed me that if I let things about one type of person build up inside me, there's no telling what I will do. It showed me that I should be more in tune when I encounter different races. . . . It has helped me grow as a young African American female and show that not all of us are thieves. . . . I also learned that if I want someone or expect someone to know about my people, I should, in return, know the same amount, if not more about theirs.

Julie's response represents more accurately what was by far the consistent perspective prevalent among the vast majority of my students at the end of our inquiry. Unlike Betty and Lavonya, Julie and most of the other students, although not convinced that they had it within their locus of control to diminish racism in their lifetimes, did acknowledge that the process of inquiry had opened them up to the possibilities of continued dialogue with themselves and others on issues significant to their needs. This dialogue, in the tradition of Freire, would enable them to eschew the easily won comforts of their first impressions and, instead, seek multiple perspectives on complex issues and take responsibility for furthering that dialogue themselves. What we see in the responses represented by Julie's vignette is willingness on the part of a majority of the students to acknowledge the threat inherent in the process, but to transcend that threat via continued inquiry. By showing a willingness to "be more in tune" and to know "the same amount, if not more" when she encounters other cultures, Julie indicated how inquiry into culture will be part of her repertoire when negotiating contact zones and borderlands.

Such inquiry will allow Julie to transcend the feelings of threat she may encounter as she crosses cultures. For example, Julie's first assertion intimates that by working more closely with peers on these issues, she came to see that not everyone was as idealistic and compassionate as she, and that her world view had been complicated in pragmatic, but upsetting, ways. As Teisha's mother had worried about her daughter, Julie's somewhat sheltered view of the world had come under threat by our discussions. She realized that some of her peers were capable of making uninterrogated statements about racial and ethnic issues and that, perhaps a more threatening concern in her mind, some were unwilling to interrogate those stances when given the opportunity. In addition, this inquiry had somewhat threatened Julie's sense of self. She had come to the realization that she had the capacity for violence, that unrelieved despair and a marginalized sense of hope could cause her to be swept up in anger and rage similar to that which raced through Crown Heights in the hot August of 1991.

Despite this sense of threat, Julie used her inquiry to see herself and others she might encounter in the world as partners in a complex series of transactions, with each transaction one that shaped her and one in which she shaped others. Those transactions could shape her in ways that debilitated her or they could lead her to the authority that would allow her to take more control of her life and open herself to dialogue with both the mainstream center and others who might be marginalized. In doing so, she could present herself as someone in a growth process who interrupted the stereotypes that might seek to pigeonhole her.

Perhaps most important, Julie had allowed herself to come into contact with ideas, actions, and beliefs that created some degree of threat within her and had used the experience to grow intellectually and perhaps emotionally. Rather than retreating into the safety of the world as she had already constructed it, she moved to investigate a new iteration of that world, one that was and would continue to be under construction. As Freire and Pratt assert, Julie had risked herself in a classroom and, in doing so, had suffered both pain and pleasure in the process. Neither was a permanent state of existence and both facilitated her further inquiry into these issues beyond the frame of this project. Out of a sense of imbalance, she had found a way to feel good about herself and to project herself in a positive light. She had used the inquiry as a means to transcend the threat to her present stance. By dialoguing with other cultures—some of which were represented within the classroom—she was taking some control over her future and transacting in ways that showed authority, confidence, and openness.

MAKING SENSE OF OUR THREATENING EXPERIENCE

It is my belief that a classroom geared to support inquiry and critique, when it is functioning well, teeters on the fulcrum of threat. There is no avoiding that. The nature of the work, coupled with the prior experiences of all stakeholders, creates varying degrees of threat within us all, individually and collectively. I could call this feeling discomfort or some other term that is less "hot button" in nature. But in my mind, to do so is to devalue the importance of the emotion and therefore relegate it to some educational backburner.

For me, discomfort is what you feel when you wear a sweater on a day that turns too warm, or it's that pins and needles feeling in your leg when you've been too long behind the wheel. However, when teachers shy away from controversy in the classroom, parents ask for changes in their children's curriculum, or students construct a new sense of their world view, some aspect of their lives has come under some degree of threat.

What happens in the face of threat makes all the difference. Educators can deny its existence, shrink from it toward some relative position of safety, or inquire into it and thus transcend the feeling. As suggested by the image of the fulcrum and teeterboard, our ways of contending with threat can lift us to new heights of understanding or drop us on the seat of our pants in frustration and even dread.

It has to be noted, however, that most public schools allow no structure for this kind of deliberate and sensitive inquiry to occur. Furthermore, in efforts to reify middle-class values, discourses, and attitudes, schools tend to tolerate some feelings of threat to the exclusion of others. For example, far too many schools prefer not to raise significant questions about race because they make many White stakeholders feel threatened. However, by not raising those questions, educators daily cause many children of color to feel threatened by the silence. Why is the latter tolerable although the former is not?

In addition, there are few, if any, incentives for teachers to take risks and to investigate topics of controversy. In fact, in the high-surveillance atmosphere and hegemony of fear being fostered by many school boards through the use of content standards, high-stakes testing, and attacks on the tenure system, most teachers feel threatened and thus compelled to adopt what Freire has critiqued as "banking models" of education rather than risk censure or even losing their jobs. Instead of supporting the kind of talk that leads to the nuanced inquiries discussed in this study, most public schools take a food and festivals approach to multicultural issues. The upshot of such surface-level celebration is that the celebrated are reduced to a range of clichés, and students of the mainstream feel no real sense of urgency that impels them to understand other cultures at a deeper level.

Instead of ignoring issues that threaten, we need to pursue them through inquiry. Our ongoing dialogue into issues of race initially threatened the stances of students, parents, colleagues, and me, but then facilitated our mutual inquiries. Specifically for Rachel, the student teacher who helped plan, implement, and document this inquiry, the study raised many questions about the ways the personal and the academic transact and how the lines between one's role as teacher and one's right to privacy blur. But perhaps Rachel says it best when she notes that the Crown Heights work, although daunting and upsetting, was necessary and worthwhile. As she wrote in her journal:

At one time, I think that this notion of the political in teaching translated to me giving kids my views on the world, and intentionally or not presenting my views as the "right" way. As exhausting as the Crown Heights work has been, it has illustrated to me the benefits of providing opportunities for further exploration rather than providing right answers. I have heard and read some pretty racist and anti-Semitic stuff in the past 2 months. While my gut reaction may be to tell a student just how wrong they really are, I can already see the benefits of restraining this reaction. If I believe that the most powerful meanings are the ones made by students themselves, then I have to be the kind of teacher who will challenge their beliefs, not discount them. By the way, I am in no way claiming that this is easy—these moments are some of the most difficult I have encountered this far.

Even in coming to some sense of resolve about this work, there is an acknowledgment on Rachel's part that feeling threatened by the process is somewhat of a given. What Rachel has learned is that teachers need to give students the opportunities to make meaning for themselves and to express their beliefs about the world, no matter how hard it might be to listen to those beliefs. However, as educational philosopher John Dewey[7] argues, the role of teachers is to bring their greater maturity and experience to the classroom in order to help students to interrogate those beliefs. For Rachel, it is not where students start, and not even where they end up—for who knows where the process ends. What's more important is where they are going as we ask them to join us on these intellectual and ethical journeys and how they intend to get there.

To put this in personal terms, I have been enacting a critical inquiry stance on teaching for over 15 years, but I still feel threatened by my own practice. I don't feel threatened enough not to practice and I feel the rewards of such practice far outweigh my sense of threat. However, I'm not sure if all teachers possess my luxury of choice. At the time of this study there were a number of factors running interference for me in terms of allowing me to somewhat more easily work through my sense of feeling threatened by circumstances around me. First, I was a veteran teacher with more than 20 years experience who had established a reputation for dependability and innovation. As one of three founders of the SLC, I had carved out some space among colleagues that granted me a degree of insulation from quick and superficial critique. Fortified by leadership roles within the PhilWP and my doctoral work, I had a developed a dialogue between my practice and theory that helped to quiet the uncertainty and doubt brought about by the sense of threat around me. Unlike many new teachers or those whose circumstances have made them less confident, I had accumulated a degree of capital that provided me with more options when presented with threatening situations.

However, whatever capital I've accumulated does not make me either immune or insensitive to threat as it manifests itself in my classroom. The fluidity and unpredictability of such a place, two aspects that give inquiry such potential, still worry, scare, unhinge, and even freeze me at times. Additionally, as junior faculty in my department, whatever status I accrued as a high school teacher has been lessened at this level. It's not that it doesn't count, but it counts less here and consequently I reconsider the role of threat as it plays out in my practice.

I further argue that those who teach and do not feel at least some twinge along the continuum of threat perhaps may not be conducting inquiry. I'm not making a case that all participants in inquiry classrooms should be a jumble of paranoid neuroses, but I am saying that it seems insensitive to ask learners to interrogate their own stances as well as those of others and those of the institutions around them, without understanding that these learners might feel threatened by the activity. The sheer unknowns of the inquiry leave all participants open to potential pain and struggle.

So those of us who muck with various forms of inquiry-based pedagogy have to resist the reflex to seek a too easily won comfort and instead, as hooks, Pincus, and Pratt urge, embrace that which feels threatening, open it to investigation, and learn from the process. On a visit to Taliesin West, the architectural learning community dedicated to the legacy of Frank Lloyd Wright, I was reintroduced to one of Wright's design principles—alternatively referred to as squeeze and release or embrace and release. In either case, the principle is realized in low and tunnel-like entrances that open into wider, higher, fuller spaces. Entering into an inquiry classroom where critique is expected is much the same. One is first squeezed by the complexity and threat of the issues but, through experience, may come to see that squeezing as an embrace, and through close investigations may win the fuller and deeper spaces of understanding that await.

7

Learning as Aaron

(with Aaron Green)

She wore a niqaab—a full veil—which, for the uninitiated, seemed to say, "Keep your distance."

But her eyes reached out from the space between her veil and head covering and said, "Bring me the world."

She often covered her hands with gloves, an old-fashioned touch for Western eyes. Yet she proudly displayed her new Reeboks, gleaming white under her gown.

Her father named her April, but her sisters in Islam call her Hafeesah.

She would rise in mid-afternoon to go to the old storage room we had set aside for her prayers. If I chanced upon her in the hall after prayer, she often took these moments to kid my solemnity or single-mindedness.

As a teacher I have always been committed to presenting my students with the full spectrum of options before them, urging them to seek the most from the world, to see education as a means for pursuing their individual rainbows and challenging the status quo. But equally, I also have always been committed to respecting the beliefs of my students, to allowing them to understand their own needs, to giving them the room to bring who they are into the classroom.

April, my veiled student, was torn between her faith and her curiosity. She thrived on learning like few I have taught, yet that very learning was a threat to the orthodoxy she wished to maintain. As her teacher, I was torn between my wanting her to consume the banquet of literature before her in great gulps of enthusiasm and my deep-seated belief that her faith was an integral key to her identity.

She was an African American adolescent woman robed in the Islamic religion. I was an Eastern European middle-aged male loosely sweatered in a belief that humans could survive without God if that were to be our fate. She reached out for her education with her eyes and her voice, both clear despite the veil. I could only reach back with the same.

I thought I knew all the rules, all the moves, all the approaches for reaching students. She changed the rules.

She wanted her education as much as she wanted to observe her faith, which frowns on too much secular interaction for women.

I wanted her to experience the world as much as I wanted her to find a niche in that world that allowed her to keep the essence of who she was. So we talked. When we could, we talked. Sometimes we wrote. Sometimes in my room. Sometimes in long strides down the hall. We talked. We listened to each other. We knew that the answers were in the engagement. We knew that the engagement was the answer. We talked.

We learned to accommodate each other. She lived by the letter of the Qu'ran. She felt she could not appear provocative before men. Presentations in front of the class put her into a sticky situation. We talked. What does it mean to be provocative? In her eyes, seeking the center of attention would be unwise. Plus we could not photograph her. Yet, I taught English, and learning to speak before groups is part of English.

So, we made room for difference and found ways for her to present so we both felt satisfied. Once I had her discuss her work during lunch to a female audience and a female colleague. Another time, I left all the women students in class with my student teacher and I escorted the young men to another room. No one squawked. From that point, when April's turn to present came round, the young men in class headed for the door without my prompting.

When I asked April to take part in some professional development with the school district and student teachers, we developed discussion groups dependent on interaction of all group members. In this manner, she could contribute as she does in class discussion, without feeling that all eyes were on her. She found ways to have her say without dominating.

She never used her faith to avoid work.

She only—and always—tried to find ways for her education and her religion to co-exist.

And she accommodated me. In my zeal to expose her to the wonders of the world, I sometimes forgot that I could not—must not—expose her.

Plus, I could not deny my Western ways. In a context vocabulary exercise, I equated polygamy to aberrant thought. She said, "Hmmm," a

*"hmmm" loaded with portent. So later I pursued and later she revealed.
"Do you really think that way?" she asked. I admitted that monogamy
seemed so ingrained in Western culture that I hadn't thought twice about
the extreme negative connection I was making. Her eyes saddened and
were downcast. My only barometer. She sighed. We went on.*

*April was class salutatorian, but she did not go to graduation. Her
own choice. Going violated her principles. The ceremony was to be
videotaped. Sitting up front with the Honor Society would have put her in
a provocative way before men. Delivering her salutatorian speech was out
of the question.*

*I was divided about this decision. So was she. Yet she remained
resolute.*

*I told her as we discussed her options that, either way, I would be
sad. "If you miss graduation, I'll be upset that you denied yourself the
celebration you deserve," I said. "But if you go to graduation, I'll be upset
knowing you compromised your principles." She nodded, and her eyes
listened behind the veil.*

She made the choice she could live with. She did not attend.

*She left soon after for Bryn Mawr College. She wished to be a
gynecologist. As usual, she opened herself to learning within the frame of
her gender and her religion.*

MAKING MEANING

When I left my teaching position in the Philadelphia School District to become an assistant professor, friends created various commentaries on my
leaving. Among those, colleague Geoff Winikur generated a "Top 10 Reasons Why Bob Is Really Going to the University of Georgia" list that was
published in the PhilWP newsletter. Knowing my penchant for titling articles
that include the word *learning* (e.g., "Learning from Laura," "Learning with
April"), Geoff suggested that one ulterior motive for my heading southward
was to complete my "field research for his newest project: 'Learning from
Scarlet.'"

Taking the moment to reflect on my own experiences as a teacher and
what that might mean, I wrote, in the same issue of the newsletter, that
shifting from secondary teacher to secondary teacher advocate would be
difficult because for over 20 years I had "defined myself as teacher, as someone who saw the classroom as his reason for being and engaged students in
meaningful dialogue about the nature of our mutual existence." I went on
to note that "all my identity is wrapped up in being a teacher and I do not
shed that identity lightly."

Ultimately for me, learning to become fluent in literacy—to be a reader, writer, speaker, and listener of the word and the world—is to really become more fluent in understanding the selves we are becoming and what that means in relationship to the rest of the world. By coming to read a range of texts in a range of ways, learners continue to develop a more complicated sense of who they are in relation to others. Our ability to make meaning of texts, with text defined broadly, enables readers to learn more about who they are even as they learn how that "who" relates to cultures that surround it.

I came to see my relationship to students and our time together in the classroom as a series of transactions, ones in which learning was occurring not only for the students, but also for me. As Mary Smith had demonstrated, Marsha Pincus had reminded, and Oscar Hammerstein had lyricized, "That if you become a teacher, by your pupils you'll be taught." As we constructed our learning frameworks and came to make meaning of the texts before us, my students and I, through our mutual transactions, were coming to make meaning of, even as we were generating anew, the text of our lives.

In this chapter I focus on one student, Aaron Green, and the ways in which he used literacy, both serendipitously and with intent, to shape his emerging identity. Just as important, I discuss ways in which he and I connected within and without the classroom and what those transactions meant for both our identities. In doing so, I argue that the nature of relationships between students and teachers have much to do with the nature of the learning that occurs between them.

THE STORY OF THE QUESTION

My interest in knowing more about how Aaron used literacy to shape identity began when I noticed that he had adopted a number of pseudonyms (e.g., Zades, Genesis). Since this use of aliases is a large part of hip hop culture, I originally found these names no more than curious manifestations of adolescence. But when Aaron began to insert pages into his written work attributing the final product as property of "Madaz Publications, a subsidiary of Madaz Incorporated," I was fascinated by what I saw as a combining of hip hop culture with corporate U.S. culture, one that reflected the uneasy alliance between rappers and their recording companies.

According to Aaron, the name began when he noticed that Saddam, as in Saddam Hussein, becomes "mad as" if pronounced backwards. As he noted:

> In addition to the simple understanding that "sadam" spelled backwards is "Madaz" with the "z" sub for "s," one of my rap names was actually "Sadam Backwards." That was my second name. I went

by it the most before I went on hiatus. I think this also supplies my immature "beat around the bush" or "ongoing enigma/complex thought process" desire to make my reader or listener think when I am speaking.

But constructing the name Madaz paralleled a deliberate construction of identity, one that resulted in Aaron seeing himself as Madaz Incorporated with productions, technology, and publications as three subsidiaries, each related to a corresponding subject studied in school. In a very concrete way, Aaron had seized upon his literate identity as an intended means of expressing and making meaning of his life. This led me to wonder about the many ways Aaron had evolved a range of identities and the ways both I and literacy transacted with those identities. I became particularly interested in ways these various identities allowed him access to the mainstream culture of power and yet allowed him to create an identity that didn't feel co-opted by that culture.

Taking Aaron's "incorporation" as a cue, I began to wonder how else he had used literacy to construct identity and what role I might have played in that construction. By looking closely across Aaron's collected work in my possession, I named a number of identities based on evidence I saw in his writing. Some of these identities were fairly obvious and hinged somewhat on common cultural roles. For example, what does it mean to be a Black adolescent male living in North Philadelphia? Each of those descriptors—Black, adolescent, male, North Philadelphia—configures a range of identities in which Aaron participated. Each identity was part of larger, evolving whole. However, because his race, gender, age, and even growing up in a certain neighborhood were beyond Aaron's control, his initial participation in their evolution was largely involunatry.

However, there were other identities in which he had taken a more voluntary status, ones to which he could more actively aspire. Three identities in particular—those of provocateur, mainstream writer, and outsider—not only turned up frequently within the body of his work, but seemed to be part of ongoing dialogues that were important to the construction of Aaron's overall sense of himself. As a point of clarification, I use the term *provocateur* to mean someone who is open to and perhaps even delights in taking on perspectives that provoke strong emotional responses in others. By *mainstream writer*, I refer to writers who have accepted as at least part of their writing repertoire the basic conventions of essay writing as they are taught in most high school and first-year college composition courses. Finally, I use the term *outsider* to mean people who for whatever purpose find themselves outside some mainstream group, yet seek some advantage of that position.

The common denominator across these identities was that they allowed for voluntary control over degree of involvement; for instance, one can choose to be more or less provocative. By the time I met him, Aaron was already creating these identities. Whatever role I played, it was one of further shaping that which was already in process rather than imposing a new possibility from without. The fact that Aaron, to varying degrees, opted into this identity work created an opportunity for him to get a greater sense of his own participation and that of others. Furthermore, I don't suggest these identities as general categories, psychological, sociological, or otherwise. They merely represent useful names for identities as I saw them manifesting themselves within Aaron's greater sense of self.

TAKING AN EXISTENTIAL VIEW OF IDENTITY AND LITERACY

In "The Myth of Sisyphus," existentialist Albert Camus projected an existence that seemed devoid of meaning and reason, yet he argued that, given such circumstances, we had the capacity to bring meaning and therefore hope for our continued existence to our lives. In *Literature as Exploration*, Rosenblatt[1] described a means for exploring literature that based meaning on transactions between reader and text, and signified what these transactions might mean for understanding one's life in relationship to the wider social world. Through the work of the former, individuals grasp a sense of the human need to make meaning. In the latter work, learners are given insight into where to look for that meaning. Through the work of both educators, I construct a view of meaning that suggests it is derived from transactions with texts.

Through literacy, we come to understand ourselves in relation to the world around us. This making of meaning goes beyond decoding and comprehension because it expects students to come to understandings of themselves as individuals occupying a range of social spaces. When educators invite students to take greater cognizance of the literate world, we are inviting them to enter a process that asks them not just to acknowledge the world as others have configured it, but to make meaning of that world for themselves. At the same time, this process also allows them to place themselves into various juxtapositions with that world.

From an existential perspective, one quality that defines our dignity as humans is our capacity to engender understandings of ourselves and our world even in the face of attempts to nullify those understandings. As Lewis Gordon,[2] a Caribbean American philosopher, argues, such struggles with issues of existence are indications of an existential perspective. Using that definition, to be human is to be an existentialist. However, for people who are marginalized or oppressed, this need to examine one's identity and humanity in a context of dehumanizing pressures is all the more critical. If, as Camus suggests, living in the modern world strips all of us of our humanity, then those who confront their oppression daily have all the more reason to realize their identities as cogently as possible.

This look at Aaron's literate search for identity, then, is built upon the existential belief that humans have the capacity to be makers of meaning who strive, through literacy transactions, to create individual and collective understandings of themselves and the worlds they inhabit. In considering my classroom in light of this existential perspective, I imagine the ideas of Delpit, Freire, and Rosenblatt transacting in interesting and complicated ways. As Freire suggests, we read the world before reading the word; and the world is a text from which, as Rosenblatt discusses, we make individual meaning. By looking closely at Aaron's transactions in my classroom, by considering how he structured a sense of self in relation to the world around him, I also came to a deeper understanding of the existential importance of his literate life.

THE RAP, THE ESSAY, AND THE OP-ED PIECE

Upon entering my classroom as a ninth-grade student, Aaron distinguished himself in two ways almost immediately. The first is that he was very willing to dialogue on almost any subject and could carry on at length, even if his arguments sometimes rambled. Second, Aaron showed strong ability to express himself on paper with originality and vibrancy, if not always with coherence. He was never shy about speaking out or encountering challenges, and seemed to take particular delight in raising questions or defending stances that might provoke others to deeper thought. Despite or perhaps because of this willingness to stand outside the norm, he was well accepted by students and teachers alike and seemed as comfortable hanging with adults as he did with peers. Proud of both his African American heritage and his ability to appreciate a range of cultures, Aaron read widely in both fiction and nonfiction and listened to a range of popular music as he tried to broaden his sense of self.

Wow! model student... [handwritten marginal note]

Over the 3 years that I taught Aaron and later as I continued to serve as his mentor, I had many opportunities to read his written works, both those that I assigned and those he initiated. In looking back, these works offered clear indications of the range of voices sheltered within his burgeoning identity. My intent in this chapter is to use excerpts from three of his written pieces to show the way in which three identities—the provocateur, the mainstream writer, and the outsider—transacted with each other in these works and how Aaron used these pieces to develop those identities. On the surface, the works are so different they seem to have been written by three different writers. However, closer examination reveals a dialogue of existence that threads its way through these written works and also is revealed in Aaron's transactions with me.

The Rap

Consider first this excerpt from a rap written by Aaron as a tenth-grade student. He wrote this piece in response to an assignment about creating visions of the city. The excerpt is jarring in content and language, and, like all excerpts in this book, has been rendered "as is."

> *The enemy had changed shape*
> *Was a hero in a big cape*
> *Finally gripped and turned me from my stomach*
> *I felt my heart plummet*
> *(Background: Oh now you done it)*
> *I don't know yo*
> *Felt a drill go up my asshole*
> *My eyes saw a blackhole*
> *And drifted into it*
> *Woke up in a hot sweat*
> *Laying in bodily fluid*
> *My alieness beside me*
> *Naked*
> *With no eyes or titties*
> *A hole with a 5-inch diameter replaced her pussy*
> *I jumped out of the bed*
> *Which dislodged her head*
> *It fell to the carpet*
> *Which was coated with serpents*
> *Death was the target*

Complex in structure and theme, the rap assaults the audience with lyrics that are as compelling as they are disturbing. Brutal, sexual, and graphic, the images are of violation, alienation, and mutilation. The language is at once juvenile and sophisticated, derivative and creative, raw and refined.

The Essay

Now consider this second piece of writing, this time by Aaron as an eleventh-grade student in response to an assignment that called for reflections on and insights into the impact of the Harlem Renaissance.

> The Harlem Renaissance was, as I have adapted the thought as have many of my peers, the link between the horror of slavery, to the glory

of the Civil Rights movement. I can easily relate this event to the sequence of change that a newborn chick undergoes.

Slavery was equal to the horrific laying of the egg from the abdomen of the hen. Beautiful in its human-like order, yet terrible in its reality—a body slashing from living flesh.

The Civil Rights movement should be easily seen as the chick examining its surroundings, bending its borders, struggling for new grounds, aspiring to exist where he finds comfort, yet still realizing that there is a bit of dependence that he has to the greater power.

The Harlem Renaissance fits perfectly between those two events[,] perfectly chronologically as well as logically. One has to become before he can advance as one. And this here, is the cracking and hatching of the chick from its defenseless egg.

Get it?

This rendering, too, is a complex and image-rich selection. The language use and structure show a different kind of sophistication when compared with the rap. A driving metaphoric image is sustained at length. The ideas discussed intimate a depth of knowledge of the subject. Yet, to Aaron's credit, the essay manages to evoke the somewhat sardonic voice and personality of a 16-year-old student even as it shows marked command and control of the essay form.

The Op-Ed Piece

Consider one more excerpt, this one written when Aaron was a freshman at a small liberal arts college in the northeast. This writing was intended to be an op-ed piece for the institution's newspaper, with the primary purpose of showing how too many students at this college were "arrogant people who have no idea as to how the ideal smaller environment should be [run]."

Intelligence comes in about as many forms as vehicles. And, actually, intelligence is comparable to cars in more qualitative ways too. For instance, every car in its youth can get you from practically anywhere on land to anywhere else on land; and intelligence can get you anywhere in our society to practically anywhere else in our society. And as the car ages, its capability to travel lessens—although a positive diagnostics could get it back up to where it could perform virtually parallel to its untouched state. But let's not include diagnostics yet, and say that eventually the car grows sour.

Intelligence works in a similar fashion. And just as cars depend on several independent factors within its engine, intelligence depends on several factors including guidance and attitude. We have all had guidance towards a better living condition in one form or another. Some of the guidance that we are issued is not understood until after its significance has expired and we're knee deep in our own blood, puss, manure, and vomit, imagining unsuccessfully that the level of which is not rising . . .

Graphic yet earnest, chaotic yet methodical, this excerpt, like the one before it, begins by working a metaphor, but then spins that metaphor through a range of permutations. What began as a controlled discussion soon slips down several asides before erupting into purple images that leave readers wondering how they got there.

PUTTING IT ALL TOGETHER

Despite their surface differences, all three pieces share stylistic details that indicate their common source. Some readers may have picked up the similarity in language use and, to an extent, voice. Yet, these writings also present vivid contrasts and conjure up starkly dissimilar images of identity. Rather than being exceptions to the bulk of his writing and thus representing anomalies or extremes, this rap, this essay, and this op-ed piece are fairly common examples of the range and types of writing that Aaron shared with me regularly.

As Aaron's teacher and mentor, I was confronted by the many challenges his work presented. Before me, and evident in all three excerpts, was a writer of uncommon creativity. His facility with language eclipsed his years, and his capacity to push his thinking beyond superficial and common argument also marked a maturity of critical insight not seen in many adolescents. Yet, he held a fascination for the grotesque, violent, and apocalyptic. How could I, and was it within my purview to, foster this originality and yet channel at least some of that energy toward subject matter that was more celebratory of the human spirit? Furthermore, his constantly associative mind often made for writing that, although vividly descriptive, spun off in more directions than most readers would want to follow, the resulting draft resembling more a maze of interesting, but only vaguely connected, ideas than a path to understanding. How could I, if he agreed, help Aaron to temper some of that inventive association for the sake of a firmer authorial stance developed through cohesion of thought?

Yet, the cost of such focusing couldn't be a stifling of his wonderfully creative voice nor could it represent a shifting away from the identities Aaron wanted to develop. For example, I had to wonder whether the writer represented in the essay was becoming more disciplined or more indoctrinated. As Delpit suggested, this negotiation of Aaron's writing needed to be about celebrating what Aaron brought to the class as well as giving him choice regarding his acquisition of the power codes. For me, putting this theory into practice meant acknowledging the complex ways Aaron's various identities manifested themselves in his literate work.

The Provocateur

One of the identities that Aaron seemed to embrace was that of provocateur. Evident in all three pieces discussed here, as it was in most of his writing, the identity of provocateur seems most readily accessible in the rap. Written as a means of representing the violent nature of city life, this rap is one piece in an anthology of original and published pieces written and compiled by Aaron and three peers as a response to an assignment to create a literary compilation that gave insight into some facet of city life. Aaron and his group decided to create an urban landscape called Violencopolis, a place where, "Higher office officials/[are] Killed with micro-missiles," and where, "If you won't pay attention/You get killed." In contrast, most of the other groups picked themes like "love and the city" and "work and the city."

The rap, 68 lines long and titled "Bad Dreams," depicts a nightmare gone awry, one in which reality and fantasy blur. The excerpt is fairly representative of the graphic nature of the whole as well as of the overall tone, language choice, and themes. The narrator seems to have fallen down a rabbit hole of horrors that Lewis Carroll, if he ever thought of such degradation, certainly never wrote about. At points in the rap, the narrator is funneled excrement, finds himself in a room "decorated with green brains," and has his testicles smashed. The piece ends with the narrator questioning, "Was it/ Torture?" and responding, "To me/ It was soothing/I love the smell of flesh and blood removing,/From one another."

It was perhaps Aaron's identity of provocateur that I found most troubling as a teacher. That he could take my breath away with his creative ability was evident from the start. That he also could cause me great worry with what he chose to write was evident too. As noted, Aaron could render descriptions that were as terrifying in their depth of vision as they were terrifying in their carnality and gore. I found the misogynistic overtones and glorification of violence in the writing to be off-putting. On the other hand, Aaron's ability to sustain image, manipulate language, and evoke emotion were to be admired and supported. Both aspects of his work—the repellant and the provocative—were part of his literate identity. Could I accept the mainstream writer without the provocateur? Could I support the one and not the another? If I moved to neutralize those aspects I found off-putting, would I also neutralize the creative zeal that drove the writing in the first place?

Interestingly, this piece represents a dialogue between the counterculture world of hip hop and the writings of such arguably mainstream writers as Stephen King and Clive Barker. At the time of this writing, Aaron was drawing heavily on both rap and horror genres. Of the latter, he notes in this interview excerpt:

> I read a whole lot. My favorite author was Stephen King. Stephen King is the man because he's a more mental writer. He gets real deep. I love it when I have to make myself think complex thoughts. It's like different levels of thought that the brain goes through at certain times and it adjusts. You know what I mean? But Stephen King, he just like got in me. So, after reading Stephen King and having the ability to get those thoughts in my head, I started writing myself.

The affinity for Stephen King is evident here, but also, as Aaron related, reading King and others invited him into a world of deep and complex thought. It provided him with the confidence that he could make his own meaning and share it with others through writing, an activity that replaced reading in priority for him because it allowed him to create a world to which he could relate. It may be an unintended play on words, but it is apt that Aaron characterized his move toward authorship as "I started writing myself," as if writing to construct his identity.

Rap often became his medium of expression, partly because a large part of the culture of adolescent urban Black working-class males in the 1990s revolved around the listening to, writing, and performing of rap. It was not uncommon to stand in the halls of my school and listen to "beats" emanating from young men passing by, or catch clusters of young men at lunch trying to outdo one another's rhymes. However, I sensed that the choice went deeper for Aaron, in that he saw rap as a way to position himself, as hooks[3] suggests, on the margins of the mainstream in order to call mainstream values and issues into question. Aaron sensed a certain alienation from a range of cultures, as will be discussed later, and, I believe, saw rap as a way to use his outsider status to his advantage.

At the same time, his writing reflected his sense of what it meant to be a mainstream writer, and showed knowledge of meter, format, and literary devices. From his perspective, he was writing from the literary tradition of Stephen King as he depicted the violence and gore that often would so appall me—especially when he wanted to use such writing as part of his application for summer enrichment course grants or college applications. On the other hand, his writing also projected his positioning as an outsider. He used the genre that such politically active groups as Run DMC and Public Enemy have used as a forum for critiquing the racist attitudes and policies still inherent in U.S. society.

All of this was done in service of his identity as a provocateur. Writing was the way he concurrently handled his own demons and yet held a mirror up to the world to witness its own cruelty. As he noted about writing in this interview excerpt:

> But I think that writing is the way that your brain has a no-holds-barred way of expressing itself. You know what I mean? Cause fiction or nonfiction, it's just the way it is. . . . If I'm mad or if I had the urge to kill somebody, or if I had the urge to rape somebody, then I can do it in my writing. You know what I mean? I can do it through writing. You know what I'm saying?

As far as I can tell, and what I deeply believe to be true, Aaron's capacity for violence and horror remained fixed on the page. I never witnessed Aaron to be either violent or disrespectful to women. Unlike some of the other young men I have taught, I never had to pull him out of scuffles or suggest he apologize for inappropriate behavior. His writing, instead, reflected an ongoing discussion with these issues, one that he eventually talked through and left behind.

The Mainstream Writer

Perhaps the identity I most consciously nurtured in Aaron was that of mainstream writer, probably for two reasons. The first is because it was where I felt I could provide the most insight. He came to me fairly well read in the categories of horror and science fiction, but was less broadly aware of the greater range of genres. His fluency and grasp of language obviously were nourished by that steady diet of reading. Yet, as often is the case with creative writers, Aaron's writing could be simultaneously about everything and about nothing. Too frequently, his process would cause him to touch on so many ideas that, although all showed great promise, the parts never gathered to a powerfully cohesive whole. It was in this area of bringing some measure of discipline to the creativity that I actively sought to work with Aaron. Along with whatever identity of mainstream writer he was constructing, I wanted to include some sense of control over the writing process.

But the second reason involved my own writing roots and intentions as a writer. Coming from a working-class family, I have my own love/hate relationship with mainstream codes. On the one hand, I enjoy the great possibility inherent in the classic essay tradition and the ways close attention to detail in the use and placement of the written word can intensify the depth of transaction with the reader. Yet, I also know and distrust the ways such discourse can draw the soul out of the voice of the writer, leaving the prose much too distant in stance and anonymous in style. To remove the writer so thoroughly from the essay or research, in my mind, is to create a false sense of objectivity and dispassion. It also creates fairly deadening text. Therefore, although I wanted to invite Aaron into this tradition of mainstream academic writing, I wanted him to come in on his own terms with his creativity not only intact, but enhanced and aware.

The essay excerpted above was one of his most controlled pieces of writing for me and it occurred after we had been conferencing about his writing for 3 years. It was part of a much larger portfolio of work that pulled our 3-month inquiry into issues of the Harlem Renaissance toward some cohesion and meaning for each student. In the portfolio, Aaron elected to generally discuss the effectiveness of the Harlem Renaissance as he saw it, to reflect on what he came to learn through this investigation, to discuss several works from that time period that held meaning for him, and to critique his own performance as W. E. B. Du Bois during our Harlem Renaissance Fair. The excerpt is taken from the first page of a five-page overview.

My written comments on the entire portfolio for the Harlem Renaissance work reflected the 3-year transaction Aaron and I had had regarding what I construed as his need to take more control over his writing, particularly as he considered more mainstream academic genres and audiences. Knowing that I was leaving for a university faculty position and that this was probably the last substantive piece he would share with me as my student, I wrote, "Thank you, you could not have given me a better parting gift. It shows you taking control of an essay without losing the essential you. You got it!" Those words sum up what I had been trying to help him accomplish in terms of a mainstream writer identity—to be both an insider and an outsider regarding the discourse and to use that outsider stance as provocateur to push the conventions to wider inclusivity.

I can't say that I didn't resort to using all my conferred institutional authority to bear upon these transactions about control that often pivoted around some piece of Aaron's writing that we were discussing either officially, as part of class, or self-initiated by Aaron. At times, I could be heavy-handed in these transactions, as Aaron, in a piece he initiated, described one of our writing conferences.

His shoulders rose to his ears as a half second preparation for,
"You're rambling on." He pulled his sleeves to his elbows taking
them from the mid-forearm positioning of yester-second, then
proceeded in forming a cup with one hand, as the other ran through

the brown hair of his head. "It sounds a lot like your fiction." He attempted another facial gesture as he temporarily set his eyes on an object outside of me, then peered back at me with, "Use that wonderful talent of description that you have and tell a story. Don't ramble on about nothing." He paused just long enough to let me acknowledge his disappointment in me, then he returned to me with "Just do it." He'd expected a lot out of me this time; if anything is the consequence of our extended relationship, let that be it—his high expectations for me. And it was accepted.

I know that to some this may not seem to be much of either a negotiation or an inquiry. Clearly I'm doing all the talking, I'm being fairly evaluative and didactic, and there seems to be no room for Aaron. Also, much of my language is packed with assumed meaning. Perhaps the most troubling part of this description for me is that Aaron interpreted part of my affect as that of disappointment, and I can't say that I wasn't feeling that emotion. Although I try not to feel disappointment regarding student effort—I find the emotion often carries more weight than it should—I had come to expect more from Aaron and most likely felt he owed us both more effort in this piece.

I'd have to say that what is written above is a fair description of some of our meetings. But so too is this depiction of another conference conversation, written by Aaron within the same descriptive piece.

He and I were sitting discussing an essay that I had written as part of an inquiry assignment that was assigned in class—he showing me "me" and how I function, for I sometimes lose track of my internal purpose, [which] is to [relay] my ideas to others in a way where they can understand what I'm saying. He and I usually sit and chat, not only about school, yet about other things that I erect, or issues in society that he and I share or would like an outside opinion of. As I have stated before, we have had a consequential extended relationship and in the midst have gained a volume of trust between us.

What Aaron described in this second excerpt—this "consequential extended relationship" of trust developed through numerous dialogues over time meant that I seemingly could be heavy-handed, as in the prior excerpt, and neither lose that trust nor have my words seen as anything other than strong suggestions meant to challenge him as a writer.

It was in this same atmosphere of trust that Aaron was able to share writing that challenged my sensibilities and my sense of the appropriate. As is evident by the language used, we were talking not just about Aaron's writing, but also about our mutual perspectives on his identity. In developing this space and time where he could see himself through my eyes, we co-constructed a process of trust that freed us both to take risks that would serve to push ourselves even as we pushed one another. He saw himself as a writer, I saw him in like terms, and our relationship was able to proceed in complicated ways through that acknowledgment.

The Outsider

If the provocateur in Aaron caused me the most consternation, and the mainstream writer was the identity I most consciously cultivated, then Aaron's stance as an outsider is the identity to which I could and can most relate. Having been placed into a position as outsider at various times throughout my life, I had intimate understanding of how the outside can be, as bell hooks[4] has described, both a position of marginality and one of power. It was this latter construct—of viewing one's degrees of being outside the mainstream as a way to access power—that I became most interested in and could most relate to Aaron's identity as outsider.

Aaron's writing was about making a place that felt comfortable to him, that represented his sense of himself as opposed to others' sense of what they thought he should be. Aaron enjoyed a wider range of music than many of his peers; in addition, his interest in literacy was a quality shared with but a small circle of friends. For these and other reasons, he felt uncomfortable in both the mainstream and his local community, feeling that he fit completely in neither. His frustration centered around both Black and White depictions of African American life. As he wrote:

> Because there is a lot of wonderful Black authors out here and they don't . . . a lot of them don't write to what I respect . . . I was thinking to myself that I don't really fit in [my community]. I don't fit into no groups. I don't think I fit in. Or whatever society I fit in, I'm not in it. You know what I'm saying? But then every author that comes out reflects the normal urban society of everybody, being like the majority of the people being into drugs. And then you got your whores on the side. Then you got that one female that's telling everybody they should be in school. Or you got that one old man that's giving knowledge to the whole world. I don't see that reality. I'm sure there's people out there that do. But I don't.

Unable to find a reality in his reading that spoke to his construction of the world, Aaron instead took to writing his own vision. Part of that vision was a graphic fantasy world that reflected his interest in shock literary genres, but part of that vision was imagining a world of ideas and dialogue. As he explained:

> I used to be a person that [said], "I'm just going to keep that to myself." But when you keep things to yourself, you hurt yourself as well as the rest of the world because they say you only come to this world once and I believe the same thing. . . . So, but anyhow, I just think people should let people know what's up. Some people, you don't want to talk to because they're not going to really hear what you're saying or when you say it, they're just going to say something negative about it. You got to sift through those people and you have to touch other people because some people don't really have any idea about the world. I don't mean to say that they don't know what they are talking about and they don't have any ideas about the world. . . . I just think people should speak their mind and there is not enough people doing it.

Aaron embraced the importance of dialogue, but he sought a dialogue that allowed for the interrogation of self as well as the interrogation of others. Part of Aaron's frustration evident here is his encountering people who, rather than engaging in dialogue, speak only to make pronouncements or attempt to censor their views rather than speaking their minds. In our SLC, Aaron had begun to develop a cadre of peers and teachers who were open to dialogue, and he saw himself as, at least to some greater degree than he had before, fitting into school.

The op-ed piece shows his eventual frustration at losing that sense of community and once more being pushed into rather than selecting an outsider's identity. Written completely at Aaron's initiative in response to the college newspaper's editorial requests for commentary on school life, this four-page, single-spaced work raises important questions about the experience of Black working-class students at colleges that serve primarily middle- and upper-class White students. Pushing language use through word play and choice, it is simultaneously academic and conversational in discourse, focused and rambling in scope, inviting and off-putting in tone.

All three identities discussed here—provocateur, mainstream writer, and outsider—present themselves in this work. In fact, the provocateur surfaced in the first sentence of the piece in which Aaron acknowledged that "since high school, at the least my peers have known me as one willing to stir the pot of my surroundings." Having raised his provocateur identity to a metacognitive level for both himself and his reader, Aaron then argued essentially that the vast majority of students at the school were so into asserting only themselves and the mainstream culture that they were completely unaware of the possibilities for dialogue across culture that a small learning community might hold. He suggested that these students "only involve themselves in conversations so they can relay how much they need not be told," and that they ought to remember what they "have learned about conversations and have one for a change." His sense of alienating the reader was so keen that a third of the way into the piece, Aaron wrote, "If, however, you are still reading this article," the person might be the kind of caring and involved student he was trying to reach as an audience.

Despite the tangents he indulged in and the hard line he evoked, Aaron also used all that he had learned about writing a mainstream essay. Even the parts of this op-ed piece that one might consider tangential or off-putting still show a sustained focus and development of argument. And once the argument he was constructing got underway, Aaron worked at sustaining it, as this excerpt notes.

> I believe that intelligence has more to do with experience and the capitalizing off other's experiences. And intelligence is, in more ways than one, a community driven phenomenon—this is why the human belief in intellect is still surviving in the first place.
>
> From what I have come to understand, a small community, such as [our school] has more to do with the involving of all of its participants, than staying with he who can easily reminisce. This isn't a vast communion as is the case with colleges such as Penn State or (insert small-city-size state college here). In a community as we have [here], there shouldn't be a such thing as alienation. Maybe, from another angle, we have things such as non-empathetic individuals much too concerned with their back, that they aren't considering how much they front.

Aaron knew the genre and its variances well enough to use them to his advantage and to experiment. He was using writing to further his ideas rather than the reverse, using a list of ideas to further his writing. The former activity shows a level of maturity and confidence in the process of writing that the latter activity comes nowhere near approaching.

Yet, more than anything else, this op-ed piece planted Aaron squarely as an outsider, the position he chose from which to write his paper and the perspective with which he clearly aligned. He wanted nothing to do with the student majority who, according to him, lacked the needed sensitivity to enact a true learning community. The irony is that having come from high school learning experiences that capitalized on building community in substantive ways, Aaron was capable of seeing the lost opportunity at his college. Acknowledging this lack, he took a stance outside the mainstream in order to draw the attention of that group to his issues. Simultaneously using conventions mainstream students would recognize, but using language and raising issues that forced them into a perspective that was less their own, Aaron carried his readers beyond the relative comfort of the center and invited them to view the world from the margins. In doing so, Aaron managed, at least for a time, to create a shift in the power relations that had been working against him.

SEEING THE WHOLE STUDENT

Reading and writing are so much more than reading and writing, or at least as we traditionally construct them. If children go through school seeing their literacy transactions only as classroom assignments—something to be done in school because the teacher has required it—and little more, then we essentially help doom them to unexamined lives. When we ask students to make meaning of a story through either reading or writing, we really are asking them to make meaning of themselves in relation to that story and ultimately to the world they live in. They are constructing identity. The more complex the dialogue, the more complex these identities and the individual's conception of the world with which those identities transact.

Through close examination of Aaron's work, we see this existential process in action. He was very aware of the ways literacy gave him insight into himself and the world around him. As he mentioned, writing allowed him to explore impulses that, if acted on, would take him into territory no longer sanctioned by the majority of society. Reading, on the other hand, helped to stabilize him. As he said in an interview:

> But reading is just the way that you recognize the normal. You know what I mean? It's like reading is your light to the gateways. I mean you can take the right way, you know what I'm saying? . . . That's what I see reading does. Other than the normal things like gathering information and stuff like that, reading allows you the norm.

As Aaron expressed here, reading and writing had a push me/pull you kind of relationship for him. In his cosmos, writing allowed him to tempt the fates, to entertain that which is taboo, to consider the inconsiderable. On the other hand, Aaron saw reading as a stabilizing force in his life, almost a conscience, one from which he could come to understand the mainstream or, as he typified it, "the norm." If writing propelled him outward from the center, reading tended to reel him in.

This complexity of tensions and identities transacting in multiple ways drove me to the root of my pedagogy and raised questions for me that, if left to my own devices, I might have never examined. In this way, Aaron was like other students I have written about (Laura and April) in that his presence in the classroom created a tension within my pedagogy of which I was forced to take notice and into which I felt compelled to inquire. In effect, Aaron's exploration of identity through literacy enabled me to further explore my various teaching identities.

As my transactions with April and Aaron indicate, these tensions played out in a range of ways and raised different questions for me. With April, I wondered how far I could nudge her into more secular exploration of the world around her without causing interference with her religious understandings of how to cope with that world. Could she and I accept tensions within her that had one voice calling for inquiry into the dynamic and fast-disappearing second millennium of Western culture, even as another voice within her suggested an acceptance of an ancient and Middle Eastern code based solely on faith? So with April, my hope was to pull her into the mainstream possibilities as far as her interpretation of her religion would allow her to go.

As I transacted with Aaron and his literacy expressions, my worry was that rather than being a source for expansion of his understanding of the world, as I felt was the case with April, mainstream codes, such as they were, would feel confining and limiting for him. I found myself asking whether my encouraging him to take greater control of his writing and to do it in ways that more closely mirrored mainstream writing styles and conventions was leading him toward greater acts of creativity or merely toward greater adherence to the dominant power code. Although I wanted him to develop a coherence and focus of written expression that I think bring power and depth to writing, I didn't want that to be at the expense of his fluid grace and creative expression.

The implication I take for me as I ply my craft in other classrooms is that the identities we shape through literacy need to be supported by systematic and intentional inquiry over time. We need to be aware of the tensions our pedagogy places on students and to at least wonder what those transactions mean in the immediate and long-term lives of our students. The longer I teach, the less I believe in the idea that decisions we make in classrooms are right or wrong. Instead, such decisions are on some continuum of appropriateness; there are more appropriate and less appropriate responses to situations. I think what we can expect is that teachers who transact with such a wide number of students and their cultures will be sensitive to the tensions in the classroom and to try to choose from a range of more appropriate responses.

Therefore, as teachers we need to view this reading and writing business as more than just business as usual. As we worked on developing Aaron as a reader and writer, we also were developing his sense of self and how it related to the world as he was coming to understand it. I suspect this remains true to a lesser or greater extent with all students with whom I worked. If so, then I need to provide all students with literacy transactions that are substantive and to give them the time to evoke substantive reflection from the work through substantive transactions with adults and peers. It is in these relationships, cultivated over time and through much dialogue, that inquiry flourishes. Without strong relationships built upon the ebb and flow of dialogue, teaching becomes rote and therefore virtually meaningless.

CODA

Life beyond high school for both Aaron and April has been eventful, and somewhat ironic. Although matriculating on scholarship at an elite liberal arts college was exciting for April, it also proved to be problematic. As expected, Bryn Mawr opened up worlds for April, but it also caused conflict with her more established cultures and identities. Embraced by some students and teachers, she also found herself facing more cultural differences than she had before. Curiously, her expectation of being supported by the international Islamic women's community at the school was somewhat thwarted because many of those students came to U.S. schools for an education in order to escape the kind of orthodoxy that April was trying to assume. Within her first 2 years on the Main Line, she decided to marry a former Crossroads student who had converted to Islam. I lost touch when their email began to be returned as undeliverable, knowing only that she was no longer in school, but happy because she was about to give birth. I have heard recently, however, that she has returned to her studies at the same school she left earlier.

Aaron also went on scholarship to a small liberal arts college outside Philadelphia. Like April, he, too, experienced both the excitement of wider possibilities and the frustration of not being accepted or understood for who he was or was becoming. An ongoing struggle within his family left him financially and emotionally unsupported, and this was exacerbated by his fathering a child. Having gone through a bleak period of clinical depression, Aaron left school and worked a variety of jobs to make ends meet and hopefully set himself up for a return to undergraduate status. Rather than seeking quick but dangerous solutions like dealing drugs or running numbers, Aaron kept communication lines open with me and other mentors in the Philadelphia social services community. During these times, his ability to express himself through writing enabled him to keep perspective, despite the dark thoughts he was confronting. He finally elected to marry the mother of his child and to enter the U.S. military as a means of stabilizing his finances and gaining some hope for future schooling. He continues to be in the military at the time of this writing. I can't help but wonder what all these post-high-school experiences have meant to his continued understanding of who he is and who he might be.

8

Refusing to Go Along with the Joke

Sometime in spring of 1998 Rashaad, along with the rest of the students in my four sections of English, took a standardized achievement test. A high school sophomore at the time, Rashaad was street wise and forthcoming, yet he was starting to see himself as someone who could not only negotiate academic work, but enjoy the process as well. If at times he still struggled with the completion of some work, he well understood when he wasn't giving his fullest effort and would respond with a disarmingly sheepish smile when called on these points.

In leafing through his answer booklet, I noticed he had responses that seemed out of character for him. Instead of the depth and imagination I had come to expect from Rashaad, these answers were simplistic and showed lack of thought. For example, when asked to reflect on a lesson the narrator learned in a reading that was focused around a fable, Rashaad answered, "There was no lesson to be learned from this. I think that because there was none taught." Further on, the test, in referring to the same reading, asked Rashaad to write down anything else he felt was important about the story. He wrote, "I think nothing about the story. I think there's nothing important in it at all."

Due to the manner in which the test is scored—off site and without explanation of the range of acceptable responses—I have no way of knowing for sure, but I don't believe these answers written by Rashaad were the kind of responses valued by the test scorers. Furthermore, even if the test in some way accounted for these responses in a positive manner, they in no way showed what Rashaad was capable of doing. For contrast, consider this excerpt from a portfolio he compiled on our Harlem Renais-

sance investigation, which I present with any deviance from standard
conventions intact.

> *The blacks in this time were very involved with the different things*
> *going on at that time. W. E. B. Du Bois played a major part in the*
> *Harlem Renaissance, he was one of the founders of the NAACP he*
> *believed black people would advance only by developing their own*
> *society and culture as they pressed for their full rights as citizens.*
> *DuBois's belief was supported by many, but a fellow by the name of*
> *Marcus Garvey thought differently. Marcus Garvey founded the*
> *U.N.I.A. Garvey's belief was that Black's should be totally indepen-*
> *dent socially, politically, and economically from whites. Garvey also*
> *disliked the fact that the NAACP had help from whites. I think both*
> *of their beliefs were good ones, they both made a lot of black people*
> *start believing in themselves and each other in my eyes. If Garvey and*
> *DuBois would have gotten along better many more changes would*
> *have happened.*

Despite the run-on sentences and informal language of this excerpt,
Rashaad showed he was capable of interpreting complex texts, synthesiz-
ing those texts, and responding in complex and thoughtful prose of his
own. In this writing he shows knowledge of the beliefs of two provocative
writers, compares and contrasts their views, and makes his own supposi-
tions. If you compare his responses on the standardized test to this one,
it's hard to believe both were written by the same learner.

When I asked Rashaad why he had responded as he had on the
standardized test, he said. "[The story] meant nothing. They just wrote it
so we could answer the question. The question didn't have any substance.
It was a real simple reading and I gave it a real simple answer." Regard-
ing his response to the second test question, he continued, "I understood
[the story]. It wasn't hard. There wasn't much to think about it. My little
brother would understand the story. This story is from an elementary
school reading book." In effect, Rashaad felt the test had no connection
to his academic or personal life and, furthermore, it seemed to undervalue
his interests and skills.

But I also wanted to know why the Rashaad who responded more
thoughtfully to text in my class seemed so different from the one who
wrote so superficially on the standardized test. In response to my question
as to why he answered in more complex ways to texts I offered, he said,
"Everything we read [in class] makes a point about something. We read it
because of a project we're gonna do or are doing. . . . The readings we
read mean something. We don't read them just to read them. This thing

we just read by Marcus Garvey made us think a little bit. The way it was written, the words that he used. It was a history of my people and not just written for a test. "

MAKING MEANING

In a very general sense, students can respond in three ways to how we teach them. One response is to resist, to either through passive or active means set impediments in the way of learning and/or in the way of delivering that learning. This latter distinction is important because it posits that students might resist not education as much as the kind of education they are experiencing. Resistance can be as spontaneous as acting out in class or as organized as a circulated petition. However, perhaps the most common form of resistance enacted by students is to just not do the work.

Students also can be compliant. That is, they can do the work. Many teachers see this outcome, the doing of work to completion, as desirable, and, to an extent, I suppose it is. However, I think we who teach, settle too often for compliance. Frequently, students comply, but only to get work done or done for grade, but not to do it in ways that attach meaningful purpose to it or that hold potential for richer and deeper understandings. I suspect that what passes for student response in too many schools is compliance; that, in exchange for lowered expectations, students comply with what is placed before them.

Or students can engage. I see engagement as an active consideration of content and ideas via an immersion in dialogue. Students and teachers work toward understanding based on both common and individual agendas. Reasons for learning are identified and students take multiple routes toward multiple perspectives. In all cases, engagement in learning involves more than just knowing material; it also involves critique, perspective, synthesis, and the asking of new and more complex questions. The challenge, according to Dewey,[1] is to provide learners with experiences that acquaint them with the past "in such a way that the acquaintance is a potent agent in appreciation of the living present," as well as to allow for quality experiences that "live fruitfully and creatively in subsequent experiences."

However, I see resistance, compliance, and engagement more complexly than this discussion might imply. For example, as educators Karla Moller and JoBeth Allen[2] indicate, students can be engaged resistors, actively calling a text into question, or compliance can be seen as a stepping stone toward resistance or engagement. Nor do any of these terms have an absolute value rating for me. Although I consider engagement more positively than the others, I also understand that there are times for both compliance and resistance in a classroom. Thus, the same student within the time frame of one class period might shift across all three relative states, or what may be seen as resistance in one situation might pass for compliance or engagement in another.

In Rashaad's story, we see him vividly offering resistance and describing engagement. Knowing him as I did, I wasn't surprised by the brevity of his test responses. Having worked with him for 2 years, I had a sense of what motivated him and what he valued. What he answered didn't catch me off guard as much as it deepened my concern about the relationship between standardized tests and many marginalized students. Not being engaged by the text offered in the test and having no rationale that made sense to him for compliance other than the most basic level of response, Rashaad resisted. His resistance came in the form of a description of what he was thinking rather than as a response to the question. Fundamentally, he was blowing off the test because he saw no way for the test-taking experience "to live fruitfully and creatively" in his near or distant future.

In the same year, David, the son of an elementary teacher and community college professor, took the elementary school version of the SAT-9. In talking to his mother about the test, this young man noted that some of the readings weren't important to him, but he knew what they, the test makers, wanted, so he gave them what they expected. Not long afterward David's younger brother Daniel encountered a phonics-laden, first-grade reading curriculum. With both parents being literacy educators, Daniel came to school not only decoding and comprehending, but making meaning. When asked by his mother what he thought of all this phonics drill, Daniel responded, "I know it's not really reading, but I'll go along with the joke."

These comments are from sons of educators, children who had embraced a cultural sense that sometimes in school one does what is expected and not necessarily what seems useful, logical, or purposeful from one's perspective or for one's perceived needs. I offer that Rashaad—an adolescent son of working-class parents—also knew what the test makers and the school wanted, but he refused to play by those rules. He ascribed to a cultural tenet that frowned on going along to get along. Rashaad's unwillingness to take the test for the testing's sake was just such an act of resistance.

However, I also argue that the compliance shown by David and Daniel was a form of resistance. In fact, I argue that compliance is even more dissimilar from engagement than is resistance. From my stance, compliance can indicate a more complete devaluing of the educational system. Because in compliance these young men, as do so many other students on a daily basis, essentially expressed that they would play the game of education as dictated, but they wouldn't value it. Through their comments and at such young ages, David and Daniel indicated that they wouldn't raise ripples in the chalk dust, but they also wouldn't value particular classroom literacy experiences.

These issues of resistance, compliance, and engagement as they relate to a literacy classroom and the transactions that occur there are the stuff of this chapter. In particular, I show what engagement looked like in my classroom and, of greater import to me, what it meant for my students and me to strive for engagement through our literacy inquiries. By focusing on three students who were both stimulated by but also wary of this pedagogy, I give a sense of the ways multiple inquiry transactions over time provided them with opportunities to entertain a range of perspectives and come to more complex understandings of themselves and the world around them. In doing so, I discuss the complicated ways we crossed culture, how we interrogated our own stances as well as those of others, and how we took responsibility for our own learning as well as being responsive to a range of learning agendas. The intent is to show the powerful ways we saw ourselves engaged in the work of the classroom, and also how even these good efforts left us with a range of views about how we learned, a range as problematic as it is intriguing.

LISTENING TO STUDENT CONCERNS

Having been professionally reared at least partly by teachers from Philadelphia's Teachers Learning Cooperative (TLC), I can't imagine working in classrooms without trying to understand student perspectives. Teachers in TLC have been influenced by the work of Patricia Carini and the teachers at Vermont's Prospect School.[3] Therefore, looking closely at student work, systematically observing the transactions of children in classrooms, and listening with intent to what children say, is central to TLC's concepts of understanding practice. The influence of TLC teachers has helped me to move away from traditional concepts of secondary classrooms where students are, much like serfs in a fiefdom, subject to the subject being taught. Instead, I have tried to embrace the idea that to understand schools, one needs to, at least as some part of the process, understand students and invite them into dialogue.

It seems that too many schools talk at, through, and around, but rarely with, students. I get particularly perplexed at this phenomenon because when I do, indeed, talk with students, I seem to learn so much about what matters in school, what matters to them, and how these two conceptions are both in accordance and at odds. One thing that I often find in these discussions is the disgruntlement that lies just below the surface of compliance. Frequently our strongest students are the ones with the most disdain for school. Just because students are compliant doesn't mean they either enjoy school or find it worthwhile: it might and often does mean that, for a number of reasons, they aren't going to make their true feelings known. The reasons range from fear of recriminations, to a perception that raising the issue wouldn't make a difference, and on to a sense that a good student goes along unquestioningly with the program.

Yet when given time and opportunity to talk about school, strong students often are critical. The following quotes are taken from informal interviews with a range of students from four working-class high schools in Australia. These just happen to be good examples of what I'm trying to illustrate; I've had similar results with similar frequency in schools in the United States, as I am confident anyone would interviewing most student populations being taught by traditional methods. In their words, these students express their frustration with what seems like anything other than an engaging school experience.

> "I want teachers to not treat [me] like a baby, but to treat [me] like a person."

> "I want a teacher to actually let us say what we feel."

> "The routine of school is painful."

> "We're just marking time, doing the same thing over and over again."

> "I hate work that has no connection to your life."

What stands out for me is the bluntness of the responses. These students are not mincing their words. Nor, I might point out, are they shirking their responsibility. There are no complaints here that the work is either too difficult or too great in volume. There is no appeal here for entertainment. Instead, these students seek work that breaks the routine and sameness of the classroom and challenges the learner. There is an appeal to be seen as someone who brings experience and knowledge to the classroom and to have that experience and knowledge valued. In tandem, it is hoped that what occurs in the classroom will have some immediate relevance to student life and not just the doubtful promise of paying off at some later date. These are students who, although taking a critical view of their education, are still willing to imagine an education that would be more critical. Yet there is a passivity to their words, that the learning experience is being done to them rather than with them. They have complied, but seek engagement.

My experience says it doesn't have to be this way, that when given support, respect, and responsibility, students respond in kind. Furthermore, formal education becomes something they want to embrace rather than something they feel required to endure, no more a hoop to jump through, but instead a journey to take. Consider these responses culled from reaction sheets and reflective discussions at the ends of projects during the year the SLC I was part of investigated the question, "What is change?"

> Instead of just telling us—standing in front of us lecturing—[the teacher tells] us how to go about doing it, and then gives us the freedom to go and do it ourselves. . . . When you actually do it, it actually means something to you.

> We used a lot of resources. We asked a lot of questions. And afterwards, we had our own opinions and theories on how to solve problems. And we read up on it, we wrote our own statements as to what was going on and with our task force. We, like, solved problems.

> The [learning] situation that's occurring kind of gets your mind stirred up. If there's a problem, like a door will open. You look into it.

> [An inquiry-based class] is not like a regular English class where you read a story and then you write about the story. It's like you're in the story yourself, you're part of it, and you've got to figure out a way to solve the problems in the story.

What marks these responses, particularly in juxtaposition to the earlier responses, is the energy these words bring, not to what should be, but what is. The students here talk about taking responsibility for their own learning. They revel in their ability to stay focused and to seek answers to their own questions. There is a tone of excitement about being immersed in learning. The metaphors—opening doors, being part of the story—are overwhelmingly positive, especially when compared with the pain, boredom, and infantilization that were so emblematic of the first group of responses. There is an active voice to these remarks that seems to invoke a sense of responsible power as opposed to being at the mercy of decisions by others.

What kind of classroom evokes such responses from a range of students? Based on both informal and systematic studies of my practice over more than 20 years, I believe that a classroom where inquiry transactions happen more consistently and frequently pushes all class participants to such levels of engagement. As students shape and are shaped by text, one another, the teacher, and the community outside the classroom, they come to grasp deeper understandings of themselves and how they relate to the world around them.

RECOGNIZING DIFFERENCE

When trying to send a uniform message about teaching or other classroom-related factors, it's not any one thing that delivers the message. It's everything. To help my students grasp the possibilities of taking a more active role in their education by using literacy to inquire into themselves and the world around them, I needed to create a range of classroom opportunities and structures that helped them not only to reflect on what they were investigating, but also to better understand the processes they were using in the inquiry. As April noted, this raising of consciousness began with something as seemingly pedestrian as room arrangement.

> The first thing I noticed was the way the desks were positioned. And that [the desk positioning] was not usual for a regular classroom. Well, the classrooms that I had been in. And it was usually, you know, row by row, a set way that the classrooms were aligned. The classroom desks aligned in your room was different, and I liked it because I—from that point, I just figured, OK, then . . . it's not the same as a typical classroom. So I assumed that the way that things will go on in that classroom will be different as well. Well, um, as far as the way it looked, that's the first thing I noticed. And it made me feel good because it would be different.

In this case, the desks in my room were arranged in forward-facing groups of four, eight of which were scattered in a fan-like pattern through a room wider than it was deep. This arrangement allowed for both whole- and small-group discussion—the angled quads of desks permitting most students to easily establish eye contact with most other students and also accommodating face-to-face, small-group work with only a modicum of movement.

However, physical difference from more traditional arrangements of desks in six by five grids was only the start of how I tried to signal and incorporate a different sense of learning within my classroom. To that end, structural, curricular, teaching, and assessment decisions were all driven by how well they supported our efforts to inquire into the world rather than being rehashers of what others say. My efforts were to enact change not for the sake of change, but with the intent to support an overarching philosophy that assumes that students are theorizers who in their transactions with varied texts (e.g., books, movies. music, physical spaces, peers, etc.) could and would make meaning of the world in an ongoing personal and social process.

In this chapter, I explore primarily those transactions that occurred between students and me. Although transactions with text, peers, and the community were of vital importance to how we learned in my classroom, my sense is that it was students transacting with me in rich, substantive, and sincere ways that provided the basis on which all other transactions were able to deepen and expand. However, the intent is not to foster what some have called teacher as "hero,"[4] but instead to show the complex ways teachers and students transact. The focus is on the classroom I shared with my students, but this work represents, to varying degrees, what was occurring in other classrooms in our SLC. In addition, the transactions shown here complicate and problematize what was occurring in the context of our classroom. This is not a discussion of "best practice," but an examination of complex practice.

THE STUDENTS AND THEIR PREVIOUS LEARNING EXPERIENCES

This chapter focuses on the work and responses of three students: Aaron, April, and Mark. I discussed April and Aaron fairly thoroughly in Chapter 7, but need to say some words of introduction about Mark. At the time of the interview, he was a senior and about to graduate, having been a student in my class since he was a ninth grader. I remember him as being strong-willed and even a bit cocky, and he came into the school with work habits that were somewhat lax. However, he eventually showed us that he possessed a desire to engage and a certain perseverance as well as insight to tackle complexity in text. Although he was known to be able to push some buttons of most teachers, he was also well accepted by faculty and students.

As a group, these were all strong students, although they didn't necessarily exhibit such strengths throughout their earlier educations. The fact that a student opted for Simon Gratz rather than attending one of the many academic, magnet, alternative, and vocational high schools often indicated that he or she had struggled somewhere along the academic way. I would place April, Aaron, and Mark into the category so many of our Crossroads students seemed to fall into: bright and inquisitive, but lacking either the polish or conformity to fit the narrow definition of "academic achiever" that most often "succeeded" in those other schools. Their struggles had been more with the codes of school than with the work itself. In short, each in his or her own way had refused to be compliant.

It is this lack of compliance coupled with their insight that led me to focus on their responses here. These are students who, like Rashaad, didn't go along to get along. Nor were they rude or overbearing in their resistance, at least not with me. But they did take personal stands and each, as I have demonstrated with Aaron and April, called some of my actions into question even as each appreciated other things I've done. Therefore, their responses are somewhat like those of critical friends, incorporating both the rose petal and the thorn on the same stalk. As I've indicated earlier, these are students who, through their comments and questioning, both affirmed my practice and called it into question. As I pushed them, they nudged me.

CROSSING CULTURE

Easily sitting in my chair, which was not assigned by higher authority, yet wasn't a choice of my own free choice, watching him, as the righteous, attentive student. He paced the floor. Allowing the analogy, he represented a general informing his troops; we were the newcomers. At least I was a newcomer. And seeing this white man in front of all these black kids, trying to teach—and actually succeeding—in the deeper regions of an "African American" based society, North Philadelphia, made him seem even more of a radical. He spoke freely of his physical differences from the majority of his students as if a casual thing, yet with the same free attitude he expressed the likeness between our diversities. He was another who had shined light on me; he confirmed that we ARE [emphasis in the original] our only barricades in the world—as far as society goes. Not to say that he personally implanted these things within my head for these are my own conclusions from such general meetings with him, yet to give credit he was an influence of my present view of the world.

When I read this description of me, an excerpt from a self-initiated piece by Aaron, I both smile and cringe. To see ourselves as others see us. Always startling. Always illuminating.

It's particularly hard for me to feel comfortable with the "general informing his troops" analogy. But, especially since Aaron was describing his first few days in my class, it's probably apt. As much as I believe in critique and inquiry and the value of community and negotiated norms and curriculum, I also know that the ethos that pervaded my students was one of expectations of authority. Even though they didn't like being policed in class, especially by a White man, my students saw any stance other than omniscient omnipotence on the part of any teacher as a weakness to be exploited. So the "general" in me was tugged out by Mary Smith and other mentors in my early teaching days. "You gotta start where the students are," they informed me. That meant not only cognitively, but affectively. In effect, I had only nominal authority until, by meeting their image of a fair but firm teacher, my students conferred real authority upon me. I first had to be the teacher they expected before I could become the teacher I much preferred to be.

But Aaron's description also offers insight into that teacher I wanted to be and into the complexity of trying to teach across cultures. That casualness he writes of regarding my crossing racial boundaries was not always part of my teaching persona. As this book has documented in a number of ways, I had much to learn about such issues and particularly about expressing my concerns and questions over racial matters. So the casualness was one borne of effort, focus, and many missteps on my part, a willingness to confront these issues within my classroom and within myself.

Also, I didn't seek to merely immerse myself in some essential understanding of what it means to teach in a classroom where the students are African American and Caribbean American and whose families are most often of the working class. Instead, I sought to dialogue across culture, to create a classroom where my evolving sense of myself would transact with that of my students. From April's perspective, my moves as a teacher looked as she described here.

> Well, I don't know what it is about you that makes [African American students] so comfortable with you. I don't know. You don't have the talk, you don't have the walk . . . the typical, African American, or whatever. It's not like you have to put on some type of show to get to get us to like you. You didn't have to, like, you know, wear jeans or Timberlands, or whatever. You were, you know, Dr. Fecho. And, like I said, I don't know what it is, but it's just like you allowed us to get into the conversation. You talked about things we were interested in, things that had to do with us. And you made it interesting, because you—like I said, you guided us through those skills that we wanted, and it allowed us, when conversations like that came up, it allowed us to express ourselves. . . . But we had no problem engaging in [gender] conversation, because we had been trained to do it, and how to get what we want out of the other person, their ideas or whatever. It was easy to talk, and we just crossed [boundaries] when we had to. There's something that we were doing. I'm trying to think of it—it had to do with—you drew a diagram on the board. . . . I don't know, I don't think you'll probably remember either, cause I don't remember enough about that time. But, yeah, it wasn't hard because you, like, laid out a way for us to do it, and when the time was right, we put that into practice. You know, how to talk to each other. And it was easy to cross those boundaries because we were just

being ourselves. You allowed us to be ourselves and talk. Unless it got completely out of hand or something and you said "OK, that's enough. We're going to do another thing." You just started it and sat back and let us go at it. And, you know, it was OK.

Within this rather long response, April encapsulates a number of ideas about what it means to work across cultural boundaries in an inquiry classroom: allowing for participants to be themselves, providing a complementary structure that enables inquiry, helping participants find relevancy, and building on student strengths to give insight into student needs.

April noted that I made little attempt to overtly express myself through the language and dress of adolescent African American culture. I didn't feel it necessary or even appropriate to take on their slang and fashion. I dressed, spoke, and carried myself in ways that felt comfortable to me. However, it's hard to imagine teaching long in any place and not overtly and tacitly picking up the codes of that community, as I did. What April couldn't see was how my teaching for so long in the African American community caused me to create a persona that was somewhat larger than life and to be more effusive in expressing feelings than I would have been had I not taught there. Not knowing me as a young teacher, April had no way of understanding how 20 years of transactions with a range of African American discourse had evoked and privileged aspects of my own working-class background, a background I shared with many of my students, even if I didn't share a commonalty of race.

My transactions with Black culture amplified my directness, my enthusiasm for language and language play, and my range of emotional response. For example, I well understood how middle-class codes, with their implied commands posed as questions (e.g., Would you like to open your books?), were seen as requests by many of my students. Understanding the power of directness—having been raised by very direct parents—I regularly spoke with directness and thus avoided many misunderstandings. My classroom language and demeanor became a synthesis of my language experiences teaching in that community and allowed for a similar range on the part of my students. The inquiry transactions in my classroom represented an ongoing transaction between Afrocentric and Eurocentric ways of knowing, which were seen through the experiences of African Americans, Caribbean Americans, and one European American.

In addition, April noted that I created structures that helped students connect to the work and to bring their own experience and culture into the classroom. As she stated, almost matter of factly, "you, like, laid out a way for us to [talk across culture], and when the time was right, we put that into practice." Unlike some popular conceptions of inquiry classrooms, they are not sites of anarchy or relativism where, because anything goes, nothing has import or substance. Instead, the structure is a clear framework of questions and emerging theory from which further study can evolve. Such a framework allows for a range of ways for students and the teacher to bring their varying perspectives to the classroom, with all views valued as new meaning is individually and collectively synthesized.

But as Aaron, April, and other students have testified, my attempts to be open about race and other cultural issues and to inquire into race issues, rather than pontificating or spouting platitudes, paid off in the realization on the part of most of my students that such discussions could transpire across culture. April pointed out that such ethos, modeling, and structure of inquiring into complex issues made it easy for her and other students to cross cultural boundaries of race, gender, ethnicity, and the like. This was not always the case in her experience. At one point in an interview, April compared my way of working with that of another veteran European American teacher, but one who was new to Simon Gratz and for whom the students were showing much disrespect through verbal confrontations.

> I think she came in there, "OK, this is who I am, and I'm going to teach you [a school subject]. If you don't like it, then—oh, well." . . . Not that she didn't care, but she didn't want to understand why the students treated her this way. She didn't stop, you know, and try to see . . . OK, I mean. Because it was so obvious that they were just outright disrespecting this woman. I would think that she would try, "OK, see what it is, then. Let me talk to my students. Let's just—you know, put the chalk down, stop the insults. What is it?" You know, it never happened like that. It always ended up her running out the classroom, or going and calling a [nonteaching assistant] or something like that. And it's just, I don't know. And that just made it worse.

What this excerpt reinforces for me is my understanding that the "general" persona that Aaron alluded to could work only for so long. As I noted in Chapter 1 about Mary Smith, she was tough on students, but they all had no doubts that she cared about each of them. I not only had to show I cared, I had to be willing to be open for and open to my students. In bridging racial gaps, I needed to transact—to shape and be shaped—with them. Although I might have had more experience in negotiating language matters than my students, I wasn't necessarily more expert on issues of race.

It is important to indicate here that in no way am I making an essential argument that for European American teachers to work with African American students they should do as I have done to the letter. Nor do I intend to imply that I or anyone has the process of crossing cultures through pedagogy figured out, or that my own experience isn't dotted with false steps, misunderstandings, and even major collisions. What I have described here is what some of my students have identified as being effective in my boundary-crossing transactions with them. Other students and my colleagues may have different versions of the same story. Although I suspect that a range of possibilities exist for anyone teaching across any cultural boundary, I believe that my experience suggests that allowing for an inquiry stance, to intentionally gather data and to reflect on their meaning, will help teachers and students to cross cultures in ways that may be less problematic and more enriching.

INTERROGATING SELF AND OTHERS

As my students understood, one of my roles in class was to act as questioner, to pose inquiry when ideas seemed to be too easily accepted, by either the speaker or the audience. Aaron described it thus:

> It seems as though Dr. Fecho is more involved with the class. Know what I'm saying? Like he be instigating some stuff, know what I'm saying? He be talking about one thing and he say, "But why do you mean that?" Or, "Where does that come from? Explain that. Do this. Do that. Are you sure you mean this? Yada, yada, yada . . ." I be like, "Ah, man, all right, um, well," and then you have to explain yourself.

The intent was and remains to help students not rest on superficial ideas, but instead complicate and deepen their understandings. My purpose is not to impose my ideas on my students—my stances are as open to interrogation as all others in the classroom—but to help my students learn how to more deeply investigate and more clearly articulate their own evolving views. I want to help them understand that what they understand today is not necessarily what they'll understand tomorrow. If I do have an agenda and expectations that I try to assert in class, they're that my students will come to see themselves as inquirers in an ongoing process of inquiry. If they open their stances and those of others to interrogation, then I feel a need to support them in their efforts, even if their views run contrary to mine.

Expressing the intentions above is much easier than putting that expression into practice. I would argue that teachers, too, need support and practice in figuring out how to inquire well in classrooms, particularly ones where many cultural boundaries may be crossed—which is to say, all classrooms. At various times I was more or less successful as an exemplar for my students. Chapter 6 showed how such work can feel threatening to a range of stakeholders. One of the key reasons for this sense of threat is that students are expected to articulate not only what they believe, but why they believe it. Although they might be used to asserting the former, too often students are not required to essay on the latter. Therefore, students sometimes can feel hung out to dry in the quest to help them delve rather than settle. Consider this extended discussion by Aaron and Mark:

> *Mark:* Plus in this class, it helped me like, to accept some humiliation. Because if you're standing on something, and it's wrong, and somebody knock you down for it, or whatever, and—you just got to suck it up and sit there, while everybody looking like—but that's what I used to do. Every year, I used to get all mad, and start trying to do this and do that, and that would even cause things to go worse. But this class, it helped me to like, just accept it or whatever, just to get more information and stand strong on that. And just go ahead or whatever. You know? I even accept sometimes humiliation from Mr. Fecho or whatever.
>
> *Aaron:* I know, man. Oh, man.
>
> *Mark:* It just makes you stronger, or whatever. Cause you going into the real world, you going to get humiliated, you're not used to it or whatever, you [unclear] to feel dumb, but it's something to get used to. You know? It just helps you, and you just learn from it.
>
> *Aaron:* It helps you learn about your own attitude. Cause you see, getting hyped does not solve anything. It still makes you look silly, and that makes you look even more silly.
>
> *Mark:* Then you just don't know what's going on, and then you just sit there.
>
> *BF:* Tell me about a time—since you mentioned me humiliating you, and I'm curious as to what that means to you—tell me about a time when you felt that I may have humiliated you.
>
> *Mark:* Oh, there's so many.
>
> [laughter]
>
> *Mark:* But, I guess I can—one time I guess I was getting off the subject or whatever, and I was in the ninth grade, and I was getting off the subject, and I was doing little stuff in here trying to stand on my ground, but, it was—leading to it—and that's something I do now, I give information, and then somebody [unclear] on that information. And then I give them the other information that leads to it, and they'll be like, wow. And I wasn't really good in that, really, to make people fall on my background. And I was just starting out, or whatever. I had

said something, and everybody looked at me, and [Mr. Fecho] was like, "That doesn't really deal with this, or whatever."

Aaron: Oh, yeah!

Mark: And then, that caused the whole class to look at it like, "Yeah." And I was all talking, and class got quiet, like, "This guy just run off the mouth." And Fecho was just up there sitting on his stool and a girl, she was like, "So, what's the point?" And everybody stopped and looked at me, and I got quiet, cause there wasn't one. And it was all because of Fecho.

Aaron: I know, man. Fecho'll just nail you. On that same stool, with his right leg up. And his book in his lap. Whoa.

In the excerpt, I seem to be the distant professional following the leads of my informants and so coolly asking Mark and Aaron to explain further what they mean by my humiliating them because "I'm curious." Actually at the time of the interview my mind was racing in a thousand directions trying to fathom how, when, and how often I had humiliated them and what the ramifications of my actions were. Never was it my intent to humiliate a student and the thought of doing so is abhorrent to me. Yet here were students with whom I had developed close relationships and they were recounting episodes where they had felt, to use their term, humiliated.

At least part of the answer lies in differing connotations of the word *humiliate*, it having less dire consequences for Mark and Aaron than for me. The joking and laughter during this discussion lends to the argument that while I had put the young men on the hot seat, I hadn't crushed their being. To a certain extent they saw this questioning as a rite of passage, an experience that toughened them for a tough world. Although not intentional on my part, I can see how these young men would see it that way and I can live with that portrait of my practice.

That said, I had left them in places where they felt less than secure and had done this more than once. Given that they must have felt uncomfortable and even possibly threatened in these situations, I had to wonder why they were willing to continue to go to such intersections of inquiry with me. At least part of that answer lies in the excerpt. Both Aaron and Mark said that these situations helped them to learn about themselves and how to cope when circumstances shifted in ways they weren't ready to encounter. In effect, they became stronger academically because they learned how to hold their own in discussion. Their self-esteem as students was raised rather than lowered because they came to understand how to develop their reasoning, to develop an argument, and, as Mark mentioned, to "fall on my background" and develop a response instead of just shooting from the "lip."

I argue, however, that without other factors in place, such sticky discussions instead could lead students to a lowering of their academic self-esteem, that a sense of humiliation truer to my connotation could take place. As I described in Chapter 7, working over time with students allows teachers who seek it the opportunity to engender a sense of trust that will help teachers and students to weather moments of conflict or doubt. For both Aaron and Mark, we had come to a place where they understood that my intentions were to get them to look more closely at their responses, to help them see issues as multifaceted entities requiring time, effort, and consideration. As Aaron said:

> I don't know. It's like, after so long, it's just starting to become [unclear] respect, I respect your opinion of my work. I'm saying, who am I? [I have] room for improvement. So, I mean, I respect that. . . . I mean, cause you, I mean, I know I'm not the best, I know I'm not a master, and I realize that I'm growing, and I need the advice. And when it happens, like if I hear you say something. Like when I hear you say, "Explain more about [unclear] school should be taken out of everyday life," and then like, I read an editorial or some type of article, and I see their opinion, then I have all this information. I have all this reasoning. I'm like yeah, I didn't do that in my journal. . . . That's why we let you get away with humiliating us. Most of the time.

Unless that atmosphere of trust is created, the hard work of engaging students in critical inquiry can become problematic. I have misgauged—and still misgauge sometimes—relationships in my class and expected too much of some students before they have sufficiently come to terms with the need to push themselves deeper into issues and to take my questioning as an invitation to inquire and not an accusation of sloppy academics. Of course, helping students overcome years of indoctrination through learning situations where only "right" answers were accepted is a constant obstacle. The need exists to help students see a question as a possibility for growth and not a challenge to their ignorance.

This dance, as my colleague Eurydice Bauer[5] called it, this knowing when to intercede as a teacher and when to sit back and let students fend for themselves, is perhaps the hardest part of an inquiry practice. It's a dance that can never be mastered, only practiced and practiced often with reflection and systematic looking at the process, as a dancer does for countless hours before the bar and the rehearsal hall mirror. But when students can articulate some of the steps of the dance, it indicates to me that teacher and students at least are approaching a level of comfort with the process that enables more complex and intricate patterns of engagement.

TAKING RESPONSIBILITY AND BEING RESPONSIVE

Aaron's earlier description of me as "an influence of [his] present view of the world," acknowledged my intent of helping students to make meaning for themselves. He is careful to point out that his understanding that humans are often the greatest impediments to themselves was not, as he wrote, "implanted" in his head, but rather was the result of our ongoing dialogue. He saw at least part of my role of teacher as that of facilitator of his own meaning-making dialogues, a concept with which Mark agreed.

> Having anybody over you, or whatever, that's not life. Or whatever. You know, we got enough of that in elementary and middle school. Now it's like, you're sending us out, you're preparing us and everything. That's how all the teachers [in Crossroads] are—they're preparing us. . . . And that's how it is over here, you know [assuming the role of a teacher in Crossroads]. "Let's see what the outcome is, and then I'll help you. Let's see what you know so far, so we can work on what you don't know." And that pays off. And you are doing your job, you know, [you] help us when we're in desperate need or whatever, you give us the work so we can make our minds expand.

Like Aaron, Mark had come to see the teacher as a resource, as someone to go to when one is struggling or in need of support. His description also posits teacher as child watcher, as listener, as inquirer into practice. Rather than assuming what students know or don't know, teachers, according to Mark, try to understand the current situation of each child and to build from there. Perhaps more important, both Aaron and Mark acknowledge the need for students to take responsibility for their own learning. If meaning is to be made individually as part of a social process, then teachers need to provide opportunities so that students "can make [their] minds expand."

In seeing my classroom as a place of multiple and simultaneous inquiry transactions, my concept of how I related to students changed radically from my original and more traditional conceptions of literacy teaching. Instead of seeing the classroom as a setting where students acquired a knowledge base, I began to see it as a place for mutual work, a space where my students and I were inquiring into issues and content together. Consequently, I became more open to the idea that we all could play a range of roles as we sought to make individual and collective understanding.

This accepting a range of roles did not mean that I enacted laissez faire control over the classroom. Instead, I sought to achieve a balance, one that created a framework from which students could be creative and seek their own meaning, yet provided structure that helped to focus our efforts and my support of those efforts. However, Aaron saw my framework as more of a frame, as he described it through an interview.

> Yeah. As soon as [Mark] said that [about having freedom to learn], I thought of a prison cell that's about—that has an area of about an acre, but it's still a prison cell . . . a one-acre prison cell. Cause it's like, you have mad room—you can do—you have a lot of space to pretty much do what you want to do. But then if you go too far, then you realize that you're on the perimeters, and you can really go no farther than that. So, I mean, it's like a contained freedom. Know what I'm saying? . . . It's like, you can, especially like on creative pieces, I mean you have freedom, BUT if you go beyond a certain line, which I did a couple of times, then you realize that, and Dr. Fecho will tell you that he doesn't—he's not aggressive with how he tells you, but he tells you.

As was frequently the case with Aaron's responses, this one is complex and encompasses a range of interpretation. He posits that within my classroom, there was, as he puts it, "mad room" to explore his own pursuits, but there were discernable boundaries that I politely, yet firmly, patrolled.

Do I really want my classroom depicted as a "one-acre prison cell"? Well, no. From a literary context, I'd prefer being compared with Holden Caulfield, a centerfielder of adolescence keeping students from the abyss. As metaphor, why not use my idea of an inner framework or scaffold upon which only so much outer construction can occur before the frame needs reinforcing? Or I would like to be seen as teacher as haiku poet "riding loose in harness" through the allotted 17 syllables of my classroom.

But to Aaron, I at times must have seemed like the border patrol or prison guard because it was necessary for me to define the limits of our literary exploration, although those limits were probably wider than might occur in a majority of classrooms, as he pointed out himself in a different part of the same interview.

> [Doc Fech is] not a spandex teacher, one of those tight teachers, you can't do anything else, [where] it's always like, either this form or not. Cause if that was the case, I'd probably still be in ninth grade, man. Seriously. I'd probably be in ninth [grade yet] if he was one of those tight, spandex teachers.

However, what I think Aaron also acknowledged was that the limits weren't arbitrary, that they were clear, that they were respected, and that they were negotiable. Furthermore, they were intentional. Although I have concerns about Aaron's choice of metaphor, I think his insight into the structure and intent of my pedagogy is dead on. I saw and continue to see my classroom as a place where the freedoms and responsibilities of all participants are negotiable. It is an irony of education that often the best way to help students understand their limitless potential is to help them first come to grips with limits, not in ways that constrain, but in ways that allow them to experience freedom within relatively safe and always expanding confines. Mary Smith would expect no less of me.

Upon reflection, it seems that two kinds of structure were at work in my classroom—the skeleton-like inner framework from which students would build outward and a wall-like outer perimeter that gave students some sense of how far they could build. My hope is that this outer frame, as opposed to the sturdy inner framework, was like shoji screens in a traditional Japanese household—substantive enough to define space, yet translucent and easily reconfigured. Students came to understand that Crossroads teachers would set the outside parameters, but we would set them wide enough so that they could find their own space, time, and questions within those parameters. Thus, students could take responsibility for themselves up to a point, knowing that along with their agenda, we also were negotiating the teacher's agenda as well as that of the wider community.

Talking about this room to find one's own access to and responsibility for the work of the class, Mark argued:

> The freedom [the work] gives you is that you set your own time and everything as to how you want it done. . . . And once you get everything, you got the freedom to learn about it or whatever on your own. And then that is also, you don't have a lot of freedom. Because you got to make sure everything is getting done. . . . There's actual time limits. . . . Because if you go to Dr. Fecho's time limits . . . [the work] might not be what you want it to be, but you really have no more time left. And if you set your own time limit, which he helps you to do, because you realize that with his time limit . . . then [the work] not going to be how you dreamt it would be when you first issued it.

In this response, Mark provides evidence that counters concerns by educators that teaching through inquiry is structureless, that opening classrooms to questioning creates anarchy. Instead, something more complex and interesting occurs. Students begin to take on responsibility for their own learning by setting their own parameters within the wider parameters of any given inquiry project.

Additionally, this response from Mark hints at the rigor of critique and inquiry, offering evidence to argue against conservative criticism that critical inquiry classrooms can be too permissive and lax in expectations. With freedom goes responsibility, and all students in Crossroads classes needed to gather evidence from a range of texts to make meaning for themselves. This sense of responsibility for their own meaning making was described by Mark.

> I would say, like you get your work, you do it yourself, and you use the resources you have, such as the teacher, other students, the library that Mr. Fecho have in the back of the class, old projects that we had before, the library, the Internet. It's just you and your work, you know. And that's that. Just you and your work.

Despite Mark's claims that "it's just you and your work," his response also indicates that learning was very social, with many opportunities for students to transact with adults, one another, and a range of texts. Ultimately, however, if I had 30 students in a classroom, I expected 30 different interpretations of what our mutual inquiry was helping us to come to understand. Mark and the other students in my class were expected to use a range of resources to interrogate their own stances as well as those of others. As Aaron remarked, "You can make your own decisions, but you just got to make sure you can back them up."

All participants in an inquiry classroom need to maintain a flexibility, a responsiveness to an ever-changing situation. They need to recognize, as Lindfors suggests, when an inquiry is taking place and toward what that might lead. Teachers and students need to be willing to play a range of roles and to slip in and out of those roles as the needs arise. Therefore, everyone in an inquiry classroom, to some extent, should have an awareness of what is occurring and be able to act upon the insights that self- and group monitoring might reveal.

Such responsiveness can and frequently did occur quickly in my classroom, very often coming in answer to events happening around us. When rap artist Tupac Shakur was killed, we devoted time to examining the ways his death was portrayed in the media and what was to be learned through the various versions we encountered. Students found and read a range of accounts of this young man's impact on popular culture and the way his death reflected upon "gangsta culture." Through both oral and written discussion, they commented on topics such as image cultivation, stereotyping, and journalistic integrity. As noted by April in an interview:

The assignments, of course, were very interesting, because you always incorporated what was going on around us into what we were doing. Not so much sticking to a generic syllabus for an English teacher. We were always involved in our work. And when we did . . . the assignment on Tupac Shakur, you know, it was like—OK, obviously [Dr. Fecho] didn't think about this way of going about this last year. This is something that he said, "OK, [Tupac's death] happened and I'm sure my students are affected"— not that you thought this way, but this is what I was thinking— "My students are affected by this, so what would be more interesting than to talk about something that actually affected them. They would be engaged." I mean, the strategy that you used was very— it's good because that way, like I said, no one was left out. Because of course, [Tupac's death is] something that touched all of us. Because, you know, this is our environment. This is what we know about, and I don't know—it was interesting. And at the same time, we were learning about English, but we were learning about it in a way that did not seem so—you know, it was—it involved us, and we were learning in the process.

April spoke to how this assignment was responsive to the context of the classroom on many levels. She first pointed out that such changes were to be expected in this classroom, and the rest of her comments indicated that she felt students appreciated such shifts. However, she also indicated that we were not sacrificing the learning of language arts in the process. Instead, we were engaged in a process of learning, that the personal, the social, the current, and the academic were being combined in the classroom in ways that engaged her and, she insists, engaged others.

As she continued talking about this concept of learning as a process, April discussed the ways in which students needed to be responsive to a range of learning strategies, that the learning wasn't predicated on facts culled from a book or lecture.

Because, you know, we learned about the working class through engaging with other people, like interviewing people, and finding out about what people thought. It was better than actually being taught it or reading about it in the book. Even though we did do some of that. But the main point was that we learned—I don't know—we learned through interacting with other people. And I think that was the most interesting part to me, about your whole class, that we always spent time using different routes to learning about things. It's not just something taught at us, or learning through a textbook.

What stands out to me in this excerpt is that at least some students saw the importance of learning through a range of avenues and they were open to the probable uncertainty this registered among them. Learning was no longer a discrete activity to be done in routinized ways. Texts were no longer just the books they read. Information no longer came only from the teacher. Instead, learning became something sought after via engagement with the printed word, other class participants, and the community beyond the school.

I have used the term *classroom participants* frequently in this book. I see it as an inclusive term for teacher and students, but one that doesn't necessarily reify a single role for each of those designations. In an inquiry classroom, roles blur and both students and the teacher need to be responsive to the learning needs of the group. As April saw it, that meant all participants getting involved in the process.

> It was like everyone was engaged in whatever we were talking about.
> It's not like a teacher was in front teaching something to you and
> [students] weren't involved in actually what was going on in the
> class. And I think that's good in the way that no one feels like
> they're—I don't know—left out. Because it's all—it's like a circle.
> We're like, all together in this. You know, you have your—
> [Dr. Fecho leads] the discussion and it just goes about the room. I
> really like that about it, because it's not what I was used to. And I
> actually found myself, you know, looking forward to the class and
> getting a lot out of it, because—I don't know—it's a different way of
> learning. You know, it wasn't the same as getting an assignment,
> doing it, and that's it. Talk about it, or learn about and that was all.
> It was more like, you know, we—I don't know—we were teaching
> ourselves under the guidance of a teacher.

Again, April spoke to the need for inclusiveness, for the voices of everyone in the classroom to not be "left out." Her image of a circle is interesting, because we rarely formed an actual circle in my classroom. However, in her mind's eye, we were like a circle, forming a whole through shared ideas and responsibility. The goal of all this responsiveness, as April saw it, was taking the responsibility for our own learning, the kind of learning that came through engagement more than through compliance or resistance.

SO WHAT?

It's not as if issues of crossing culture, of students taking responsibility for their own learning, of classroom participants calling their own stances and those of others into question, and of being responsive to learning situations, are discrete categories. Very little in a classroom of inquiry and critique is so distinct. That's why I both immerse myself in and am justifiably cautious of this pedagogy I practice. An inquiry classroom seeks to discern the connections, make better meaning of the blurred areas, and problematize the possible as it nudges all learners toward collaboratively constructed but individual interpretations of what is being learned. Such efforts are highly rewarding, but also carry risk with them, in some ways greater risk than traditional classrooms. If one encourages multiple perspectives, then any given facet of the classroom is open to a range of interpretations. As Mark and Aaron noted, one student's challenging moment could be another student's humiliation.

What emerges here, however, is that for Rashaad, Mark, April, and Aaron, our classroom was a place of stimulation, somewhere they embraced the hard work of learning, and accepted what that meant for them. In our work together, they began to see the importance of and ways to negotiate the crossing of cultural boundaries. Class was no longer just a place for merely doing seatwork compliantly, getting grades, and passing silently into the hall. Instead, these students saw themselves as learners with shared and distinct cultures. By opening themselves to encounters in what Pratt has called the contact zone of classrooms, their understandings of a range of cultures and of themselves became more complicated, sophisticated, and engaged. Dialogue across culture came about through all of us engaging in dialogue that helped us to be sensitive to the differences and to understand the many ways difference mattered, but also to identify what we shared across differences.

The students also understood better what it meant to take responsibility for their own education. Nor did I abdicate my responsibility to help structure that education. Instead, the students and I took responsibility and negotiated our degrees of participation. It was not acceptable in this classroom to merely copy down notes and give back information, to be merely compliant in all the passive connotations of that word. Nor was it acceptable for me to dominate discussions and always have the last word. Student voice was important, but so was that of the teacher. I have grown as wary of the term *student-centered classroom* as I have of the term *teacher-centered* classroom. I find a preponderance of either view to be problematic. I instead try to see my classroom as learning-centered, one where teachers and students continually are working out their roles and degrees of responsibility.

Another aspect of the bottom line in my classroom is that all notions were up for scrutiny. Teaching through inquiry and critique is at its most vibrant and volatile points when it facilitates interrogation of self and others. However, teachers can't forget that raising critical questions will cause students to feel and express, to varying degrees, a sense of threat. So if teachers are to encourage students to inquire and critique, they must learn to help students see threats to their perspectives as learning challenges and to use continued inquiry as a means of working through such concerns. The relationship that teachers cultivate with students must be one of trust, mutual respect, and validation. Without such a relationship, all pedagogy becomes merely steps for compliance rather than engagement.

One way to earn students' trust is to be responsive to their needs. Critical educator Ira Shor[6] has argued that three agendas are always in dialogue within any classroom: that of the student, that of the teacher, and that of the community stakeholders. None of these agendas should be ignored, but none, to my mind, should always dominate. Instead, an inquiry classroom tries to be responsive to all three agendas, creating a learning situation that allows students to feel they have some choice and voice, while still meeting needs the teacher sees as important as well as incorporating the essence of local and national standards. I don't argue that trying to be responsive to these many agendas is easy. Balance is difficult to achieve because it's always shifting. But our worry should not be whether the balance is right. Who knows for sure what that is? Our worry should be that we are trying to achieve some balance at all.

I admit that these three students represent the high end of positive response to my efforts and those of the rest of the SLC. Not all students who experienced our classrooms felt as enthusiastic and engaged about them as did April, Aaron, and Mark, nor were they all as verbal about their perceptions as these three were. I'm sure there were some students who hated coming to my class and may have distrusted me. On this continuum, however, I offer that there were far more students whose responses inclined toward the positive than the negative, and that even if April, Aaron, and Mark weren't typical in their degree of engagement, they do represent directions in which most students were heading. In my last 8 years of teaching in a public high school, all of which were spent in this SLC, more of my students were more engaged for longer periods of time. Although they could still be compliant and/or resistant, they could shift through these states of response and more easily as well as more often become engaged with depth and breadth of inquiry. If inquiry isn't the answer, it's certainly an arrow pointing in the direction that feels most right to me.

9

In Search of Wise Beauty and Beautiful Wisdom

There's something surprisingly organized about Anchorage, Alaska. Flying into the city, en route to facilitate a two week literacy institute with Alaskan teachers, I was struck by its flat and expansive stance between Cook Inlet and the Chugach Mountains, posing square and even against the irregularity of the natural boundaries. Its streets cross at perpendiculars, stretching to distance in straight lines. The downtown thoroughfares, unimaginatively labeled as numbers and letters, caused me to feel at times like some random point plotted on X and Y axes in some unfamiliar quadrant of the planet.

Maybe that's why Turnagain Arm stands out so vividly to me. Heading toward Soldotna and the group of 28 women teachers I was to work with there, I slipped over a hill, Anchorage vanishing from my rear view mirror and my windshield filling with the gray-green waters of the Turnagain, its banks full at high tide. There where the road narrows to two lanes and gently sweeps eastward, I remember being met simultaneously by the depth of silence and the magnificence of possibility. Gone was Anchorage with its bustle and predictability. In its stead, mountains, sea, and snow combined in infinite variations as far as my eye could see and my imagination could fathom. I have seen these things before—we have mountains, sea, and snow even in Georgia—but never quite this way, in such close proximity and with such a combination of power, beauty, and wisdom.

And at first it seemed very lonely—to be this small, this foreign, this faceless before this common experience stretching away in directions I still needed to travel. I wondered whether perhaps I should find the nearest

*overlook and return to those streets that, although anonymous, seemed
like I've at least known in other times, other places. Because for a moment, the mountains had appeared faceless, really all the same, a vista to
be taken as a whole. Meaning making seemed daunting, beyond my ken.
So at Beluga Point, I pulled over and set my camera to panoramic, the
lens taking in as much as it could with one breath, to prove that I had
been there, but fully intending to leave before I disturbed the quiet
timelessness.*

*But, strangely, I couldn't go back to the city, not just then at least.
Once again on the road, compelled it seemed by the wise beauty or
beautiful wisdom before me, I drove up the Turnagain in wide-eyed
wonder, curious as to what the mist would reveal if it were lifted. It was
difficult and even dangerous to pay attention to the direction I was
traveling while trying to discern particulars in that broad expanse. Somehow I caught glimmers that made individual mountains stand out to me—
a position, a frame of reference, a perspective, an attitude. Side by side, in
juxtaposition, I saw the graceful rise of one incline contrasted by the
pointedness of another. I came to know the variance of slope, the diversity
of angle, the range of texture that made for complexity of understanding.
I somehow divined that the sharp acuity of any given peak often was
tempered by a gentle face or subtle ridgeline. I saw and appreciated how
the sea and sky were not merely foundation and backdrop, but shaped
and were shaped by the landforms that rose so elegantly and knowingly
before me.*

*It is a fantasy of mine that I never really made it to Soldotna, that I
remained suspended for 2 weeks in the Turnagain, trying to read and
understand the natural wonders before me. But in truth, I safely completed the 3-hour drive and settled in beneath Redoubt volcano. From
Day One, I immersed myself in trying to understand what it meant to live
and teach in Alaska. Although I learned a lot, I never quite got the whole
of place—who could measure such an expanse in 2 decades, let alone
2 weeks? But I came to know somewhat better the features and degrees
of intensity of some 28 other forces of nature.*

MAKING MEANING

So what does a trip through Alaska's Turnagain Arm have to do with teaching about race, language, and culture in literacy classrooms? For me, one
connection is in the possibility and inadequacy of an inquiry stance. Similar
to what I experienced on this Alaskan sojourn, learners who question come
to deeper and more complex understandings of themselves and the world

around them through inquiry transactions. By asking what is this about and what does it mean, they immerse themselves in swirling channels of complexity. Yet, no matter what their depth of interest and level of involvement, they can only make sense of so much at any given time. Who they are, what they are learning, and the context within which that learning is taking place are simultaneously clarifying and blurring before their eyes. What they come to understand continually moves them to wonder about what it is that still is not comprehended. Ultimately, the process is unsettling, yet captivating.

At least part of the answer to what it means to take an inquiry stance lies in the need to see such a stance as a way of life and not just a teaching or learning strategy, an integral part of how one approaches life situations and not the next new gadget to appear on the shelves of the educational superstore. We need a perspective or stance that allows us to enter into a process and to remain within that process as we journey through life and thus our education. Therefore, taking an inquiry stance on the classroom is helped by taking a more general inquiry stance on life. By becoming learners who regularly try to make meaning of the world, we provide ourselves with lenses for looking and come to see that looking as an integral part of how we exist.

In retrospect, my inquiry stance has been evolving for a substantial portion of my life, although I wasn't always formally aware of this stance nor was it necessarily encouraged by my teachers. For too much of my formal education, all emphasis was on fact-based direct teaching with expectations of regurgitation. But if I look at the countless *Journey to the Center of the Earth* sequels I wrote as a fourth-grade student, my self-discovery of the local library, the many legal pads of poetry in my later adolescence, and other artifacts and anecdotal data, I realize that I have been using literacy fairly continuously to make sense of what I have been seeing around me. I never would have called it taking an inquiry stance at the time, but for all intents and purposes, that's what I was doing. In some "systematic and intentional" way as a learner, I was becoming a theorizer—creating theories about how the world operated, testing those theories, and reassessing.

My suspicion is that we all bring an inquiry stance to our lives, but the degree to which we do so and the awareness we bring to this activity vary greatly among us. Although I am advocating an activity—inquiring into and making sense of the world—that seems to be evident in our lives from inception, it appears that there is much in the educational, social, and political cultures we encounter that acts to suppress this. In particular, when we start our lives as teachers, the prevailing expectation is one of getting with the program on the same page at the same time of the year. Basal reading texts, packaged reading series, standardized tests, local, state, and national standards, departmental exams, scope and sequence curriculums, the eight-period day, and the like, all send messages to new teachers, and students as well, that independent thinking is to be avoided. Rather than expecting our teachers to think for themselves, we do more and more to take the decision-making process out of their hands.

Therefore, for many teachers, recognizing the need to take an inquiry stance on both their classrooms and the world around them is a complicated and anxiety-ridden process. Such a move flies in the face of most of the conventional lore generated about the role of teachers in the educational hierarchy. In addition, the embracing of an inquiry stance is neither subtle nor limited. As suggested, it requires a subsequent change in life-style, in the way one approaches and presents oneself to the world, in the way one comes to know. One of the best metaphors I can't take credit for is that of a PhilWP teacher who likened taking an inquiry stance to buying a new couch for the living room. The recent acquisition makes the rug look shabby, so out goes the broadloom. Now the walls are the wrong color for the replacement rug, the lamps are from the wrong design period, and the drapes no longer accent the overall scheme. Without the person realizing it, a process of change is underway, one that has no end in sight and is dependent on prior change. It is both systematic and serendipitous.

Perhaps this is why taking such a stance is so difficult and why such a stance should not be mandated. When we ask people to inquire into the world around them, we are asking them to enter a process, one that may involve paradigm shifts, the investment of a considerable amount of time, and a more complicated relationship with all stakeholders. Teachers who usually teach through memorization, or who are dependent on the text for questions to raise and curriculum to develop, or who remain emotionally and academically distant from their students, will find shifting to an inquiry stance difficult, perhaps arduous, probably frustrating, maybe pointless, and even anger producing, at least at first. Students who have learned well how to play to what the teacher wants, who produce mechanically correct, but intellectually bland, writing, and who tacitly agree to comply if the teacher tacitly agrees not to challenge, will struggle and often resist when asked to raise and seek possible answers to questions. Creating an inquiry classroom is hard work for those who grasp the subtleties of and intuit the need for such a pedagogy, such a way of learning. I can only see it as painful for those teachers and students who think otherwise.

Understanding the need for this perspective—for encouraging teachers and students to make meaning of their worlds via inquiry methods—is essential to making a transition from a more directed, more fact-based, more dichotomous way of teaching and learning. The deeper our sense of need for taking an inquiry stance, the greater our willingness to work toward surmounting the obstacles that complicate the transition to this perspective and its realization in the classroom. However, one thing teaching has made very clear to me is both the breadth and limitation of my locus of control. There are many factors within my circle of influence and many beyond its borders. Accepting both opportunities and limitations, I have come to appreciate that I have power to change myself and, only in starting there, can I influence others to change.

Still, I can ask others to consider change. And my belief is that as I change my own circumstances and ways of acting, others will change around me in ways that complement my actions. This chapter, therefore, ponders the changes I have observed in my own pedagogy, discusses what meaning I have brought to those changes, and suggests what my understandings might mean for a range of stakeholders. It seeks to bring some understanding to what I have discussed to date, while projecting where such work may take me and others interested in critical inquiry pedagogy.

THE CRITICAL INQUIRY CLASSROOM

There. At last, I've written it. Up to this moment, I have been dancing around a term—*critical inquiry*—mainly because, when I was teaching in the SLC, I never used this term to describe my work. I was more apt to say I ran an inquiry classroom or enacted critical pedagogy as I adapted Freirian ideas. However, neither term fully suited me. Inquiry seemed too broad and, often, too apolitical to encompass the substantive discussions around race, gender, class, and other issues of social justice that were occurring regularly in my classroom. On the other hand, critical pedagogy carried a political edge, but, as feminist educators such as Carmen Luke and Jennifer Gore[1] pointed out, too often such classrooms merely traded one dominant agenda for another, and the voice of the liberatory educator could be as overwhelming as the mainstream code.

My classroom, as it evolved, needed to be a place where inquiry took place in ways that called mainstream venues of financial, social, and political power into question, but did so in ways that allowed for a range of interpretations and perspectives. It needed to be a place of critique and inquiry. It was not enough to be either; it needed to be both. As social justice educator JoBeth Allen[2] points out, to inquire without critique is problematic, but no more so than to critique without inquiry. Furthermore, to do both and then not allow for a range of perspectives is, in my view, antithetical to the very basis of dialogue and transaction on which such work is based.

Therefore, I write this chapter with great caution. My intent is not to be definitive, but rather to be formative. This is my understanding of what it means to enact a critical inquiry classroom to this moment. Perhaps poststructuralism has made me tentative. Better that than to be frozen in time.

Critical Inquiry Classrooms Are Places of Transaction

I have come to see learning as a mesh of transactions. Classrooms are places where these transactions occur. It is important to realize or remember that transactions occur in all classrooms, that we shape and are shaped by the stories, people, patterns, sounds, and other contextual items present in all classrooms, no matter what the pedagogy. What is significant in a critical inquiry classroom is that these transactions are not only acknowledged, but inquired into. The transaction becomes somewhat of a unit of analysis. When I as teacher transact with you as student, what are the new texts we both create and what will they mean for future transactions?

Seeing a classroom as a place of transaction significantly alters perspectives on that classroom. For me, it meant that I was no longer teaching at my students; instead, we were learning together. We were involved in mutual work.

This importance of the work of school first was raised into my consciousness years ago in a talk by Patricia Carini.[3] One question she raised for all who teach concerned the work of school. If the work we do to some extent defines us, what then does it mean when we subject children to schoolwork that is rote, unstimulating, and mind deadening? When we ask students to merely reply with answers we already know, when we suggest that stories have one meaning and one meaning only, and when we as teachers do most of the talking and agenda setting in classrooms, what are we saying about what we expect from our students? How does the work of school define we who try to learn there?

By acknowledging the transactions that occur there, a critical inquiry classroom creates many opportunities for teachers and learners to be both teachers and learners and to work in substantive and life-enriching ways. Throughout these chapters, there have been many examples of the importance of these transactions. Cria and her friends, in transacting with the text created as we discussed Kenya's work, enabled all of us in that classroom to rethink our views on language. My students who voiced their reactions to the Nikki Giovanni poem used that transaction as a way for us to consider issues of language and culture. As April and I transacted around issues of religion and education, we both developed more complex views of those issues and one another. Each transaction led to even more complex and interesting transactions.

The mutually and multiply constructed texts of our classroom also changed as a result of these transactions. The work became that of authentic discovery for all involved. That discovery occurred as we made meaning of the many intricate ways we transacted. Dialogue had to take place. It was no longer only my views that counted. As we charted ideas and theories from student to student and class to class, what transacted in one class manifested it-self in more transactions in other classes. Text we transacted with in Septem-ber was still available for transaction in March. All classroom participants had the opportunity to see learning through literacy practice as a more cohesive whole, one that was connected both within and without the classroom walls.

Critical Inquiry Classrooms Embrace Literacy as an Existential Act

This is not a point to be taken lightly. From my perspective, without a will-ingness to explore deeper understandings of this concept, teachers in gen-eral, but mainstream teachers who fail to realize the multicultural nature of their classrooms in particular, will fall more distant from the adolescents they seek to reach. To make meaning is to define ourselves in relation to the world around us. To read the world and the word, as Freire told us, is not just one more catchy edu-phrase to remember. These are words around which we who teach must structure our questions, our lessons, our inquiries. We inquire to bring meaning out of chaos. Given the current state of our schools and our society, this making of meaning is more needed than ever before.

As I've noted earlier, education is not the enemy. But school might be. Even a quick glance through African American memoir will show that for males like Richard Wright, Malcolm X, and Nathan McCall, it was school and not education they were resisting. They suspected there was more to be understood through inquiry into texts than the rote drill, memorization, and racist attitudes to which they were subjected. Each found a way to embrace reading and writing in spite of and not necessarily because of school. Each used his transactions with the many texts of his life to offer some expression of himself in the face of the random yet all-too-focused debilitation that is racism.

McCall, in Rebecca Carroll's[4] *Swing Low: Black Men Writing*, stated, "I feel that a book is more powerful than a gun could ever be. It's a much better get-off. If I get mad at white folks . . . I can write something." How different is that from Aaron Green saying in an interview to me, "But I think that writing is the way that your brain has a no-holds-barred way of express-ing itself. . . . If I'm mad or if I had the urge to kill somebody . . . then I can do it in my writing"? Both men are channeling the anger that frequently comes with being raised Black, male, and working class in the United States through the interpretation and creation of complex text. In this case, the texts being created are the ones of their lives. One difference, perhaps, is that Aaron, unlike McCall, found high school to be a place that invited him to dialogue with the text he was generating rather than rejecting it out of hand.

Students read, write, and learn for many reasons. There is the entertain-ment value, the need to gather information, an intent to become citizens in a practicing democracy, a hope for financial security, and a raft of other possibilities. For many of my students, the opportunity to read and explore their own culture and that of the mainstream, and to look into both with a critical eye, is what stirred their souls. They sought to make meaning, to gain an existential understanding of their place in the world. All students need the same opportunities.

Critical Inquiry Classrooms Enable Participants to Inquire Across Cultural Boundaries

The worry of many well-meaning teachers, as they consider the multiculturalism of their classrooms, is that they are not up to the job. How does one give expression to the many cultures represented in the diverse classrooms of our time? How is it done in ways that truly value and celebrate not only similarity, but the splendor of difference? With so many cultures present, how can one teacher feel expert enough to teach them all? The teacher who has not lived as a Latina growing up in rural Georgia or a gay adolescent coming to terms with sexual identity in Los Angeles cannot be expected to be an expert on such a range of life-styles. Having lived only our life experience, we who teach can never understand fully the experiences of others, as much as we might try to empathize. However, just because the task seems formidable, should we ignore the spectrum of difference in the classroom before us and disregard how that difference matters in terms of learning?

And no teacher is free of these concerns. All classrooms are multicultural. Visitors to our SLC frequently saw only the homogeneity of race and often presumed a monoculture. But as my experience with April only vaguely suggests, I taught, and still teach, in a culturally diverse classroom. My students represented a range of religions, regions, genders, cultural histories, political stances, sexual identities, family demographics, and socioeconomic circumstances. And I was a European American male raised in a racially isolated working-class neighborhood. My students and I had much potential to cross many cultural boundaries.

Based on my experience, teaching through critical inquiry creates a flexible means for exploring culture, one that frees the teacher of being all knowing about culture, while fostering an appreciation for the many ways cultures transact. For me, this meant that I no longer had to see myself as an expert on a range of cultures. Instead, I needed to be an expert on how to inquire into culture and how to create a classroom that was culturally sensitive. So when we delved into the Harlem Renaissance, I most likely knew more than my students about the literature, but they could relate to that literature in ways I could only ponder. Nor was my knowledge of that social movement anywhere near comprehensive the first time we inquired. But I trusted the inquiry process and went in with a willingness to grow and understand with each subsequent effort.

For students, teaching through critical inquiry allowed them, as Delpit has argued, to have access to mainstream power codes while both celebrating home codes and calling all codes into question. This stance of an inquiring learner of language was particularly evident in the work of Cria, Robert, and Nora as they made sense of how they and others around them used and confronted issues of language. But such was also true as my classes delved into Crown Heights and we saw how language was used to generate a range of "truths" about the events of that community. And Aaron's involvement with reading, writing, and identity frequently led to discussions about what language to use, with what audiences, and to what effect. Language became the passport into inquiry even as it became the subject of inquiry as we crossed these linguistic cultural boundaries.

This willingness to see ourselves as learners interested in complicating and deepening our understandings became somewhat of a hallmark of our classroom. When we opened ourselves up to inquiring into language, we saw the ways our language and the language of others shaped us. As my class delved into racism and ethnism as they transacted in Crown Heights, we came to deeper understandings of how our own actions were influenced by the chasms of bigotry that still divide this nation. It was by calling our differences into focus and dialoguing around them that April and I were able to consider the mutual text we created. In both trusting and questioning my support of his writing, Aaron was able to push both of us to think anew about the existential relationship between identity and literacy. By making culture a lens through which we routinely viewed the classroom, we were all inquirers into culture in ways that deepened our understandings and connected those understandings to future work.

I grew up in a working-class neighborhood where racial and ethnic slurs were as plentiful as the sense of questioning these views lacked. My high school students grew up in a racially isolated neighborhood and, although they were forced to know more about the mainstream culture than the mainstream culture was forced to know about them, much of what they knew of other cultures was a cobbled-together mix of generalizations. There is little to be learned in the comfort zone of those two stances. My sense is that all learners need their belief structures to be routinely threatened in ways that move them to interrogate those beliefs. To do otherwise is to deny the opportunity for my students, my colleagues, and myself to teeter on that fulcrum of threat and, using our collective weight, to defy the gravity of our circumstances.

Critical Inquiry Classrooms Create Quality Learning Experiences That Foster Future Quality Learning Experiences

Much is made in educational literature of engagement in learning, of creating lifelong readers and writers, of sustaining student learning through intrinsic motivation. The why of those good ideas gets much more airplay than the how, particularly as the possibilities for such vigorous learning get pinned beneath the weight of superfluous standardized testing and unnecessarily specified curriculum. Yet the need to invigorate the work of language arts classrooms has never been more imperative. My undergraduate teaching students, learners who mostly have embraced school and succeeded there, tell story after story of how school, especially middle and high school, dredged any semblance of joy and passion from their education. They describe going through the motions of figuring out what the teacher wanted given back, of practicing their passage over and over in round-robin reading and thus never getting a sense of the whole work, of reading only the question in the back of the chapter and then finding only the subhead or paragraph that contained the factoid asked for. Far too many tell me that they did a lot of work, but they rarely had to think. And what worries me most is a significant few seem either all too content or resigned to replicate such work in the name of fear of high-stakes testing.

There is no panacea. I offer no silver bullet. That said, nothing in my experience has had more of my students more engaged more often and for longer periods than my critical inquiry practice.

The evidence is this book. My hope is that it flows upon the exuberance of teacher and students learning together. Even when students and teachers felt threatened by the work of my classroom, as occurred during our investigation of Crown Heights, the tensions allowed us to delve rather than retreat. At times of uncertainty in our exploration, some new question would get raised, as when Tai wondered, "But what is the truth?" When our beliefs were called into question, as happened to Julie, we found a way to dialogue. Despite being placed into situations within contact zones, as Rachel described so thoughtfully when asked about her religious background, we continued to inquire because the inquiry helped to immerse us in making meaning of our lives.

To sustain inquiry over time is exhausting. But it's an exhaustion borne of excitement and not of tedium. As Aaron, Mark, April, and others showed so well, school became a place that was self-affirming, intellectually stimulating, and experientially fertile. As these students immersed themselves in inquiry, they were positioning themselves for future inquiries. So as Aaron and I inquired into literacy and identity, we were able to use our histories as writers to enact mutual experience in the present that helped him to better position his future writing experiences. Simultaneously, by looking inward he came to understand more about his many writing identities even as he looked outward and sketched how those identities placed him into juxtaposition with the larger writing community. Finally, all of this inquiry occurred within my room, which was part of our SLC, which was part of Simon Gratz High School, which was in the Nicetown section of North Philadelphia, and so on. His engagement, no doubt, was the result of a range of factors; however, not the least of these factors was the way inquiry validated the experience he brought to the classroom and provided him with experiences that moved him in richer, more complicated learning directions.

Critical Inquiry Classrooms Are Places Where Learning Is Responsible and Responsive

Critical educator Allan Luke[5] has said that we are sacrificing lifelong immersion in literacy for short-term gains on tests. He worries that our current interest in high-stakes testing will create a generation of learners who may score well on close-ended tests but are fundamentally unable to lead or even follow in the changing world of this new century. In this age of high-stakes testing and mandated curriculums, policy makers often talk about holding teachers and students accountable for learning. Once again, a top-down, hegemonic, and punitive model is chosen as a means of trying to stimulate learning within school walls. Such talk implies a power relationship that sees teachers and students as subordinate in understanding the needs of the classroom. It assumes that all teachers and students are basically lazy and need some form of outside prodding in order to function. It also presupposes that whatever the general public perceives as the crisis of learning occurring in most public schools is the fault of and can be fixed by teachers and students not only acting solely on their own, but having no say about the means of reform.

Rather than holding them accountable, why don't we create ways for teachers and students to take responsibility for their actions as well as be responsive to one another? Instead of only telling them what to do, could we enable teachers and students to seek ways to teach and learn that will best serve their needs as they come to understand them? What would happen if we replaced the "hegemony of fear," as one Georgia teacher described state and national efforts to incessantly test in acontextual and close-ended ways, with a circle of responsibility, one that expected all nonteaching stakeholders to support rather than ignore knowledge generated in classrooms and the decisions made there based on that knowledge?

Taking a stance of critical inquiry creates a space where students and teachers can take responsibility for the learning that occurs there. In such a space, my eighth-period class all those years ago took hold of our curriculum and said they wanted to know more about the many complex ways they transacted with language. It was in such a space that Rashaad better understood what mattered and didn't matter to him educationally. Through critical inquiry, Cria carved out a notion of culture and language that gave her flexibility in her switching across codes. In like manner, all my classes encountered difficult issues of race and ethnicity that pointed us all in individual directions of understanding. By inquiring with an eye to critique, April and Aaron and, perhaps most of all, I used reading, writing, speaking, and listening to learn about ourselves as we learned about one another. In all these instances, the classroom participants opted for more rigorous work, frequently going beyond the expectations of the school district in efforts to develop our own understandings.

There is no aspect of a critical inquiry classroom that precludes students doing well on standardized tests. There is nothing in the way critical inquiry unfolds that would prevent good teachers from teaching reasonably conceived standardized curriculums in a quality manner. However, to test at the rate of testing we are coming to experience, to do so with the penalties we are currently attaching, and to teach under the strain of overparticularized curriculums deadens the soul and stifles the intellect of teachers and students alike. Do we want to force children into learning or do we want them to grasp the force of learning? Do we teach to assess or assess to teach? Is the intention of education to open debate or open dialogue? Again, for me, the answers lie in the creation of critical inquiry classrooms within which students and teachers take responsibility for learning based on their needs and the needs of the stakeholders beyond the classroom walls.

SO WHERE AM I GOING WITH ALL THIS?

There is a tendency when writing about the implications of research and pedagogy to speak to various audiences individually, for example, to write about implications for teachers, teacher educators, and policy makers in separate sections. I'm going to resist that tendency because, despite some arguments for doing so, I find separating these audiences largely problematic. To do so implies that a suggestion for one audience might not be a suggestion for others. It also suggests that these audiences have nothing to say to one another and that dialogue across these parties is unnecessary. In addition, by specifying audiences, we invariably leave some out. Finally, writing to separately named audiences might reinforce the already existing, but in my mind false, hierarchy that exists among these groups of educational stakeholders. So, although at times I may indicate that a particular implication might have greater weight with one group or another, in general I'll be addressing all the educational stakeholders—students, teachers, parents, administrators, teacher educators and university researchers, the business community, policy makers, and the general public. In short, all of us.

Also, for the remainder of this chapter I will use the term *learning community*. From my perspective, a learning community can be a single classroom or an entire school district and the community it serves. Therefore, what I suggest for a learning community could be enacted by a single teacher working with a single class or by a much larger and more diverse group of constituents.

1. *The first implication is that critical inquiry pedagogy must be seen as a viable choice for language arts learning communities.* Usually near mid-year, some student new to our SLC would raise his or her hand and, in all seriousness, say something like this: "Don't misunderstand. I've been enjoying all the groupwork and projects, but when are we going to start doing English?" The first time such a question was raised, I was flustered and nearly mortified until I fell back on instinct and asked of the whole class in return, "Well, have we been doing English or haven't we?" As students brainstormed the readings short and long, the writing projects big and small, the revision and editing work, the language discussions, the study and research projects, the genre inquiries, the small- and large-group discussions, the oral presentations, the listening expectations, the vocabulary excursions, and all the many other activities of our critical inquiry classroom, we were all reminded of how this classroom was most definitely about learning the language arts.

Moreover, we were learning in ways that used reading, writing, speaking, and listening as tools for learning and not as ends in themselves. What this meant is that we read and responded to *Hamlet* not because I was expected to teach Shakespearean tragedy or it was the next reading in the chronological anthology, but because the story informed us, among other things, about issues of power that were part of our ongoing inquiry. Furthermore, the work was done in context. So, for example, students read and watched a range of dramatic monologues in order to figure out the genre so that they could then write their own monologues. In both cases, inquiring into the work took longer than a lecture might have, but provided us with deeper and more varied understandings that connected in richer ways to all our lives. Critical inquiry pedagogy was more than viable in our classrooms; in most cases it flourished and helped us to flourish.

2. *If we see critical inquiry pedagogy as a viable means of educating learners, then the second implication of this work is that all educational stakeholders need to find ways to support it.* An idea our SLC learned from the

Coalition of Essential Schools[6] is that a good learning community bases its ongoing construction on a set of agreed-upon principles. This might mean adopting a set of principles like those averred by the Coalition or generating a common list of principles within a learning community. The important foundation is that those who will be most affected by the principles should have the greatest say in their creation or adoption. Then, once the principles have been agreed upon, the learning community periodically should review how well it is enacting them and make no serious addition or subtraction to the educational program without considering how it will play out with the agreed-upon principles.

If, in generating a set of principles, a learning community moves in the direction of critical inquiry pedagogy, the stakeholders must consider just what supports that work. It will differ for all learning communities and may change over time. For our SLC, it meant moving to double periods on an A/B schedule so, like 4 x 4 blocks, students and teachers got more time each day to transact around inquiry; however, unlike those semester-long blocks, we transacted for the entire year to better preserve a sense of community. It also meant changing our means of assessment by moving to more projects within courses, senior exit projects to assess what our students had come to know, and portfolios to help us see change over time. Because we expected students to analyze, evaluate, and synthesize information rather than just reproducing it, we needed measuring tools that facilitated such work.

The key understanding, however, is not so much how we changed, but that we changed. The way to support critical inquiry pedagogy, whether by an individual teacher or a whole school district, is to look ruthlessly at current structures and behaviors and determine whether they support a way of teaching that is based on questioning and exploration. In effect, the first focus of inquiry should be the learning community itself.

3. *Along with deciding how to support critical inquiry, a learning community should do all it can to make the posing of problems and asking of questions as central to each classroom as possible.* There is a paradox here. I strongly believe that teachers who have been working largely in traditional instructional ways need to ease themselves into inquiry over a number of years. To do otherwise, I feel, is to set up individuals or whole programs for failure. However, the intention of any strong program based on critical inquiry pedagogy should be to do more inquiry work more often. To do otherwise is to create a classroom where too many mixed messages are being sent about learning. There certainly are still times when I opt for more traditional instruction in my classroom, but if I can provide the time, and students can figure something out for themselves, I use activities that will foster inquiry.

Perhaps one of the easiest ways to move critical inquiry to a more central position in a learning community is to use and work from questions better and more often. One way teachers can help students self-interrogate is to simply ask for more explanation more often. Sometimes I would ask, "So what did you think of that novel?" A student might reply, " I didn't like it." Rather than moving on, I would ask, "Why didn't you like it?" More often than I would like, the student would then respond, "It was boring." The inexplicitness of the answer bothered me more than the negative reaction. "Was it?" I would wonder. "What made it boring for you?" This question functioned on a number of levels. It asked the student to evaluate and seek some sense of cause and effect. It let the student make choices, but it also implied that those choices might be particular to that individual. At this point, the student could respond, "Nothing much happens. This guy just gets kicked out of school, complains a lot, and visits his sister."

In about 2 minutes, I was able to move a student through comprehension and toward synthesis and explicitness by asking a few common questions. At this point, I probably would throw it out to the whole class in some fashion. For example, I might ask whether anyone else felt nothing happened. Such a move on my part would elicit further discussion of the novel and, most frequently, a range of perspectives on the book. Or I might ask those who liked it and those who didn't like it to write about their reasons for doing so. Then we might get into small groups, chart our information, and then analyze those charts. Nothing mystical going on here. Just using questions to help all of us use what we know about a text to learn more about that text.

Questions can be used in larger ways to drive curriculum. For example, many teachers use thematic units. An elementary classroom might study dinosaurs, or a secondary group may study the American dream or poetry. Although I think a thematic unit works to support deeper understandings of concepts, I also think such units are limited in terms of engagement if they don't revolve around questions. As Table 9.1 illustrates, the traditional thematic unit remains largely teacher-centered, while a question-driven inquiry is more apt to be learning-centered.

Finally, I no longer fear questions. In too many classrooms, students ask few questions and even fewer questions that might lead to sustained inquiry. And those questions that are asked, often are shunted aside because the teacher is intent on covering the content. As I noted above, even a query (e.g., "Is this English?") that calls the very purpose of my class into being is welcomed in my classroom, as are all questions that are posed with sincerity and allow the class to look more deeply into matters that reverberate for the group. I suspect that students have potential to ask inappropriate questions, but I also think such questions are few and far between. By making student

Table 9.1. Continuums Representing Characteristics of Thematic Units and Question-Based Inquiries

Thematic units more often . . .	Inquiries more often . . .
start as topics	begin as questions
are generated out of context	arise from the context of the learning community
have teachers doing a lot of frontloaded work	invite teachers to inquire along with their students
assume teacher as expert and student as novice	encourage teachers and students to try on new roles
emphasize learning of discrete facts	enable higher-order thinking
seek consensus of learning	seek a range of response and multiple perspectives
favor teacher preparation over student responsibility for learning	invite teachers and students to share the work and responsibility of learning
end when the unit is over	continue beyond the end of the unit because students have generated more questions to explore
remain isolated from other units and other content areas	create connections across other units and content areas

questions something all of us need to answer, rather than something only the teacher answers, we continue to reinforce the idea of a learning community where teachers and students are engaged in mutual inquiry.

4. *Another implication of this work is that all participants in a learning community need to become more comfortable with uncertainty.* This implication dovetails with an understanding that what we come to know cannot be separated from what we feel and who we are. With questioning of the stances of others and expectations of self-interrogation both central to the pedagogy, a critical inquiry classroom is fraught with potential for problematic situations. I am convinced, however, that the levels of engagement that critical inquiry brings to a language arts classroom far exceed the problems such work might provoke. Furthermore, whatever short-term uncertainty is elicited by critical inquiry pedagogy, it frequently is replaced by long-term engagement.

Although I consider it a false move to purposely manipulate emotion, I find it equally false to run a classroom as if emotion has no place in learning. Too often students and teachers in traditional classrooms are expected to leave their feelings and culture at the door, to hang them as if on hooks likes coats and other extraneous outerwear.[7] Whole courses come and go with no one ever asking how students might react to a reading, a historical event, a scientific breakthrough, or a mathematical proof. Textbook series frequently are still constructed as if all student experience and culture were the same.

Yet, if we honestly inquire into our own learning history, we most likely would see that our most memorable learning experiences were rife with emotion and the expectations of our own experience. As part of my university courses and professional development workshops, I frequently ask teachers of all ages and experience to write about an engaging learning experience from any point and place in their lives. One startling result of this work is that between two-thirds and three-quarters of these responses describe a learning experience that took place outside of school. But more to the point here, in describing these experiences, the writers use phrases like, "I was excited," "had to find out," "it became an obsession," "had to do something," "I was ticked," and other such idioms indicating desire, passion, anger, confusion, and a host of other emotions. If key learning moments in our lives involve strong emotional and cultural connections, why are many schools so quick to banish them from the classroom?

In particular, we seem too poised to exile uncertainty. The indefiniteness of uncertainty seems to scare far too many teachers and students, perhaps because, at base, we will always not know far more than we do know. But I see way too many university juniors too willing to sacrifice their creativity and possibility for a soupcon of certainty. They want me to spell out the projects we do, with some even preferring that I say, first do this, then that, then the next thing, and so on. Close-ended questioning and testing have made them afraid of giving the wrong answer or striking out on their own. Until they become accustomed to the freedom of inquiry and its potential for developing understanding, many of my students worry that they will remain uncertain.

But a critical inquiry classroom thrives on uncertainty, because in that subtle unsteadying of our confidence, the quest for learning occurs. When Aaron asked whether he could push the margins of comfort of his writing audience or when Tai wondered whether she would ever know "truth" again, they were entering into territory that felt, at the very least, unstable if not completely threatening. However, they were part of a learning community that frequently had entered such spaces and they had come to trust the process and their fellow inquirers. In fact, they eventually became so used to the process that they understood that the logical result of one inquiry is another inquiry.

5. *A final implication of my work that I choose to discuss here is the need for all stakeholders in learning communities to recognize all the possibilities of taking an inquiry stance.* It is not enough for a teacher to set students on the road to critical inquiry. As a writing teacher should be a writer, and a reading teacher a reader, so should the critical inquiry teacher critically inquire. This inquiry begins with the content of that teacher's classroom. Having taught *Romeo and Juliet* for the *n*th time, teachers should not assume they know all there is to know of that play. Instead, they should use a question to help them bring fresh eyes to a well-worn work and allow themselves other understandings, perhaps those generated by students. I always wanted to take a complex work like *Beloved* or a Greek tragedy and read it with the same class four different times, but with a different question informing each reading. Imagine what such an activity would let us know about that text, about reading, about the power of perspective.

And, if we embrace inquiry as viable for classrooms, we then need to see it as necessary for professional development and connecting the inside view of teachers with the outside view of university professors. Teachers need to be researchers in their own classrooms. As this book has demonstrated, there is much to be learned when teachers and students inquire together into the world they construct. On an individual level, I was learning more about my transactions with my students every time I collected data and reflected on them. However, I also was using those data to help others learn about their practices. By sharing videotapes of my conferences and sharing data excerpts with other educators, I informed myself, but also caused others to reflect on their own classrooms.

This sharing was as spontaneous as chats with Natalie, Marsha, and other colleagues, or as structured as presenting on a panel at the American Educational Research Association's annual conference. But, whether local or national, the discussions and reflections generated by me and by others' looking closely at my classroom have been the most powerful form of professional development in my career. Because it was driven by context and need, and because I had say over what it entailed, inquiring into my practice through various forms of practitioner and action research has empowered and informed me and my colleagues as teachers and learners like little else has. No one-shot, outside-in, administration-initiated talk-at has ever come close.

If we are to see practitioner research conducted by teachers and students as a significant voice in professional development and the research literature, then we need to recognize it as part of a teacher's job description. This also would mean that we need to create an infrastructure that would support such teacher research. Although I have been writing steadily about my practice since 1986, my output has been limited because of the traditional workload of the typical teacher. It is only in my coming to the university, where part of my time is budgeted for research and writing, that I have been able to write more prolifically about my practice. Learning communities need to acknowledge that teachers spending time inquiring into their classrooms, and sharing that work in a variety of venues, make for better teaching in general. Such work is certainly more productive than inservice days as they traditionally are conceived. Creating workloads and schedules that would allow teacher inquiry groups to flourish within a school district would move that district closer to becoming a learning community in deed and not just in name.

CRITICAL INQUIRY AS A WAY OF LIFE

In David Halberstam's *The Children*, he asserts that for some of the leaders involved in the Civil Rights Movement of the 1960s nonviolence was a strategy. It was a means to an end. It was part of a repertoire of strategies—some of them decidedly violent—that could be used in the efforts to achieve equity and opportunity for all citizens. For other leaders, such as Dr. King and John Lewis, nonviolence was a way of life. It was a standard against which one made decisions. Nonviolent protest was chosen as the means of resistance because taking a nonviolent stance on the world was key to the moral and ethical philosophy of these leaders and their followers. It wasn't an option to be nonviolent one day for one set of circumstances and to be violent the next because the circumstances had changed. To be nonviolent meant just that—to be nonviolent forever and always.

Although, in terms of righteousness and depth of significance, I in no way mean to equate the struggles of those involved in the Civil Rights Movement with the struggles of teachers trying to take a critical inquiry stance, I can and do expect educational stakeholders to see inquiry not as a strategy but as a way of life, as a way of knowing. It was easy for me, alone in and new to the Alaskan wilderness, to see the experience as a learning one in which I needed to wonder, ask questions, gather perceptions, and test theories. However, frequently we who teach and learn in everyday classrooms fail to see the same need to call educational space into question, and, as anthropologists do, make the familiar strange. In describing how I perceived and tried to make sense of Turnagain Arm, I also described how I did the same for my classroom of Alaskan teachers in Soldotna. Much as I tried to see each mountain peak for its individual qualities, I sought to better understand the stance, needs, and culture of each of the teachers with whom I worked.

This is what I ask of us for those learning communities we call schools: that we immerse ourselves in looking closely at the transactions we make across cultures; that we think about these classrooms in the shower as we prepare for work, in the car on our way there, and in our sleep, long after we have closed the classroom door; that we wonder aloud and silently, alone and with colleagues, early and late, with students and because of students; that we see the work of learners and teachers as something infinitely worthy of all this close examination; that we see the making of meaning as an existential struggle that is never completed; that we see the idea of shaping and being shaped as necessary and as impelling as the pulling of the tides; that we intuit that the crossing of cultures to dialogue within contact zones is somewhat risky, but highly rewarding; that we come to respect the intellect of every child and every teacher by expecting them to transact within rather than just occupy space. To do otherwise is to succumb to an education that is static, monolithic, and oppressive. We must see critical inquiry as a way of life, as a way of knowing. Now and for as long as such looking sustains us.

Notes

Chapter 1

1. Anzaldua, 1987
2. Pratt, 1991
3. Delpit, 1995
4. Cochran-Smith & Lytle, 1993
5. Freire, 1970
6. Rosenblatt, 1938
7. Lindfors, 1999

Chapter 2

1. Farrell, 1990; Willis, 1977
2. Anyon, 1980
3. Fine, 1991
4. Goodlad, 1984
5. Wiggins, 1987
6. Delpit, 1995
7. Ogbu, 1990
8. Shannon, 1990
9. Shannon, 1990, p. ix
10. Delpit, 1992, p. 248

Chapter 3

1. Lindfors, 1999
2. Pincus, 1994
3. Gee, 1996
4. Flower & Hayes, 1977; Shaughnessy, 1977
5. Sizer, 1984

Chapter 4

1. Csikszentmihalyi, 1990
2. Smith, 1997

3. hooks, 1994
4. Tobias, Fitzgerald, & Rothenberg, 2000
5. Atwell, 1998
6. Bakhtin, 1981
7. Rosenblatt, 1994
8. Freire, 1983
9. New London Group, 2000
10. Freire, 1970
11. Delpit, 1995

Chapter 5

1. Delpit, 1986
2. Delpit, 1988
3. Smitherman, 1977
4. Luke & Gore, 1992
5. Smitherman, 1977; Jordan, 1988

Chapter 6

1. Sorenson, 1996, pp. 88, 89
2. Freire & Macedo, 1996, p. 202
3. Freire, 1998, p. 28
4. Freire & Macedo, 1996, p. 203
5. Lindfors, 1999
6. Shipler, 1997
7. Dewey, 1938

Chapter 7

1. Rosenblatt, 1938
2. Gordon, 1997
3. hooks, 1990
4. hooks, 1990

Chapter 8

1. Dewey, 1938, pp. 23, 28
2. Moller & Allen, 2000
3. Himley, with Carini, 2000
4. Tassoni & Thelin, 2000
5. Fecho, Commeyras, Bauer, & Font, 2000
6. Shor, 1992

Chapter 9

1. Luke & Gore, 1992
2. Allen, 2002
3. Carini, 2001
4. Carroll, 1995, p. 143
5. Luke, 2002
6. Sizer, 1992
7. hooks, 1994

References

Allen, J. (2002, December). *Interrogating cultural constructs; negotiating cultural borders: Critical inquiry as a tool for teachers, students, and parents*. Panel discussion presented at the annual meeting of the National Reading Conference, Miami.

Anyon, J. (1980). Social class and the hidden curriculum of work. *Journal of Education, 162*(2), 67–92.

Anzaldua, G. (1987). *Borderlands: La Frontera*. San Francisco: Spinsters/Aunt Lute.

Atwell, N. (1998). *In the middle: New understandings about writing, reading, and learning* (2nd ed.). Portsmouth, NH: Boynton/Cook.

Bakhtin, M. (1981). *The dialogic imagination* (C. Emerson & M. Holquist, Trans.). Austin: University of Texas Press.

Carini, P. (2001). *Starting strong: A different look at children, schools, and standards*. New York: Teachers College Press.

Cochran-Smith, M., & Lytle, S. (1993). *Inside/outside: Teacher research and knowledge*. New York: Teachers College Press.

Carroll, R. (1995). *Swing low: Black men writing*. New York: Carol Southern Books.

Csikszentmihalyi, M. (1990). Literacy and intrinsic motivation. *Daedulus, 119*, 115–140.

Delpit, L. (1986). Skills and other dilemmas of a progressive Black educator. *Harvard Educational Review, 56*(4), 379–385.

Delpit, L. (1988). The silenced dialogue: Power and pedagogy in educating other people's children. *Harvard Educational Review, 58*(3), 280–298.

Delpit, L. (1992). Acquisition of literate discourse: Bowing before the master? *Theory into Practice, 31*(4), 296–302.

Delpit, L. (1995). *Other people's children: Cultural conflict in the classroom*. New York: New Press.

Dewey, J. (1938). *Experience and education*. New York: Macmillan

Farrell, E. (1990). *Hanging in and dropping out: Voices of at-risk high school students*. New York: Teachers College Press.

Fecho, B., Commeyras, M., Bauer, E., & Font, G. (2000). In rehearsal: Complicating authority in undergraduate critical inquiry classrooms. *Journal of Literacy Research, 32*(4), 471–504.

Fine, M. (1991). *Framing dropouts: Notes on the politics of an urban public school*. Albany: State University of New York Press.

Flower, L., & Hayes, J. (1977). Problem solving strategies and the writing process. *College English, 39,* 449–461.

Freire, P. (1970). *Pedagogy of the oppressed.* New York: Continuum.

Freire, P. (1983). The importance of the act of reading. *Journal of Education, 165*(1), 5–11.

Freire, P. (1998). *Teachers as cultural workers: Letters to those who dare to teach.* Boulder, CO: Westview Press.

Freire, P., & Macedo, D. (1996). A dialogue: Culture, language, and race. In P. Leistyna, A. Woodrum, & S. Sherblom (Eds.), *Breaking free: The transformative power of critical pedagogy* (pp. 199–228). Cambridge, MA: Harvard Educational Review.

Gee, J. P. (1996). *Social linguistics and literacies: Ideologies in discourses.* (2nd ed.). London: Falmer Press.

Goodlad, J. (1984). *A place called school.* New York: McGraw-Hill.

Gordon, L. (1997). Introduction: Black existential philosophy. In L. Gordon (Ed.), *Existence in Black: An anthology of Black existential philosophy* (pp. 1–9). New York: Routledge.

Himley, M., with Carini, P. (Eds.). (2000). *From another angle: Children's strengths and school standards.* New York: Teachers College Press.

hooks, b. (1990). Choosing the margin as a space of radical openness. In *Yearning: Race, gender, and cultural politics* (pp. 145–153). Boston: South End Press.

hooks, b. (1994). *Teaching to transgress: Education as a practice of freedom.* New York: Routledge.

Jordon, J. (1988). Nobody mean more to me than you and the future life of Willie Jordan. *Harvard Educational Review, 58*(3), 363–374.

Lindfors, J. (1999). *Children's inquiry: Using language to make sense of the world.* New York: Teachers College Press.

Luke, A. (2002). What happens to literacies old and new when they're turned into policy. In D. Alvermann (Ed.), *Adolescents and literacies in a digital world* (pp. 186–203). New York: Peter Lang.

Luke, C. & Gore, J. (1992). *Feminisms and critical pedagogy.* New York: Routledge.

Moller, K., & Allen, J. (2000). Connecting, resisting, and searching for safer places: Students respond to Mildred Taylor's *The Friendship. Journal of Literacy Research, 32*(2), 145–186.

New London Group. (2000). A pedagogy of multiliteracies: Designing social futures. In B. Cope & M. Kalantzis (Eds.), *Multiliteracies: Literacy learning and the design of social futures* (pp. 9–37). London: Routledge.

Ogbu, J. (1990). Minority education in comparative perspective. *Journal of Negro Education, 59*(1), 45–57.

Pincus, M. (1994, July). *Embracing the dissonance: Looking at audience in students' writing in an urban high school.* Paper presented at the summer conference of the Urban Sites Writing Network of the National Writing Project, Princeton, NJ.

Pratt, M. L. (1991). Arts of the contact zone. *Profession,* pp. 33–40.

Rosenblatt, L. (1938). *Literature as exploration.* New York: Modern Language Association.

Rosenblatt, L. (1994). The transactional theory of reading and writing. In R. Ruddell, M. Ruddell, & H. Singers (Eds.), *Theoretical models and processes of reading* (4th ed.; pp. 1057–1092). Newark, DE: International Reading Association.

Shannon, P. (1990). *The struggle to continue: Progressive reading instruction in the United States*. Portsmouth, NH: Heinemann.

Shaughnessy, M. (1977). *Errors and expectations*. New York: Oxford University Press.

Shipler, D. (1997). *A country of strangers: Blacks and Whites in America*. New York: Knopf.

Shor, I. (1992). *Empowering education: Critical teaching for social change*. Chicago: University of Chicago Press.

Sizer, T. (1984). *Horace's compromise: The dilemma of the American high school*. Boston: Houghton Mifflin.

Sizer, T. (1992). *Horace's school: Redesigning the American high school*. Boston: Houghton Mifflin.

Smith, F. (1997). *Reading without nonsense* (3rd ed.). New York: Teachers College Press.

Smitherman, G. (1977). *Talkin' and testifyin': The language of Black America*. Boston: Houghton Mifflin.

Sorenson, K. (1996). Creating a democratic classroom: Empowering students within and outside school walls. In L. E. Beyer (Ed.), *Creating democratic classrooms: The struggle to integrate theory and practice* (pp. 87–105). New York: Teachers College Press.

Tassoni, J. P., & Thelin, W. H. (2000). *Blundering for a change: Errors and expectations in critical pedagogy*. Portsmouth, NH: Heinemann.

Tobias, M., Fitzgerald, J. P., & Rothenberg, D. (Eds.). (2000). *A parliament of minds: Philosophy for the new millennium*. Albany: State University of New York Press.

Wiggins, G. (1987). The futility of trying to teach everything of importance. *Educational Leadership, 54*(4), 44–59.

Willis, P. (1977). *Learning to labor: How working class kids get working class jobs*. Westmead, England: Saxon House.

Index

About the Author

Bob Fecho is an associate professor of reading education at the University of Georgia, a position he took after teaching secondary English in the School District of Philadelphia for over 20 years. Bob is a longtime practitioner researcher whose research focus has been on critical inquiry pedagogy, adolescent literacy, and sociocultural issues. Currently, his work concerns the ways working-class adolescents construct identity through literacy and what it means to support emerging and veteran teachers as they attempt to shift to pedagogy that is more inquiry-based. Bob's writing has appeared in the *Journal of Literacy Research* and *Harvard Educational Review*, as well as other educational publications. He recently received the Alan C. Purves Award from the National Council of Teachers of English for work published in *Research in the Teaching of English* deemed most likely to influence practice. When Bob isn't visiting with his adult daughters or stepson or playing guitar in an alternative country trio, he relaxes at home with his wife, adult stepdaughter, two dogs, and cat.